CW00959127

THE BEAUTY OF BALLET

FERNAU HALL

THE BEAUTY OF BALLET

FERNAU HALL

HAMLYN

Photographic acknowledgments

All photographs supplied by the author except the following: Birgit Akesson 106 bottom; Archive der Akademie der Kunste, Berlin 69; Australian Ballet 126, 127; BBC Enterprises 146–7; BBC Television Service 61; Paul Boland 98–9; Bridgeman Art Library 21, 38 top; C.A.P.A.B./M Cooper 121; Nobby Clarke 78–9; Dee Conway 74 top, 77, 78, 131; Bill Cooper 20, 26, 28–9, 34, 75, 89 bottom, 138 left; Cuban National Theatre 112–13, 114–15, 116; Danish Tourist Board/J R Johnsen 103, 105; Zoe Dominic 16–17, 18, 30 bottom, 31, 32, 33, 45 bottom, 46, 59, 62 top, 74 bottom, 83, 87, 108–9, 110 top, 110 bottom, 122, 123, 133 top, 134, 136–7, 137, 138–9, 140–1, 141; Zoe Dominic/Catherine Ashmore 30 top, 76 bottom; English Bach Festival Trust 15; Mary Evans Picture Library 23, 38 bottom, 39 bottom; Jorge Fataures 119; Evelyn Hart 125; The Hulton Deutsch Collection 12 top, 22, 35, 45 top, 47, 48, 49, 51, 53, 54, 68, 70, 85 bottom, 97, 98 bottom, 113, 132; Robbie Jack: 10–11, 24, 25 bottom, 42 left, 44–45, 55, 56, 57, 58, 60, 63, 91, 92–3, 94, 95, 96 top, 96 bottom, 100, 101, 111, 129 top, 129 bottom, 130–1, 135; Joffrey Ballet, New York 88; Kranichphoto 142, 143; Det Konglige Teater 104; London Festival Ballet 62 bottom; Barbara Morgan 71, 72, 73; National Ballet of Canada/A Oxenham 124; National Film Archive 144, 145; Novosti Press Agency 19, 25 top, 92; Octopus Group Picture Library 27; Photo Fred Fehl 67, 76 top, 80, 81, 82, 84–5, 86 top, 86 bottom, 133 bottom; Jose R Pino 114 left; Rambert Dance Co., London 50, 52; Janet Randall 147 top left; Linda Rich 64; Royal Ballet, London 36; Leslie E Spatt title page; Sven Ulsa 118–19, 120; Victoria and Albert Museum, London 13 top, 39 top, 40, 41, 42–3, 66–7, 66 bottom; Ber Volleberg 117; Reg Wilson 89 top, 107.

Published by
The Hamlyn Publishing Group Limited
a division of the Octopus Publishing Group
Michelin House
81 Fulham Road
London SW3 6RB
and distributed for them by
Octopus Distribution Services Limited
Rushden
Northamptonshire NN10 9RZ

First published in 1989

ISBN 0 600 55634 4

Produced by Mandarin Offset
Printed and bound in Hong Kong

Contents

Tribute

to the author from Eva Evdokimova

"On with the dance; let joy be unconfined!"

My dear and trusted friend, Fernau Hall, knew so well the joy of dance. Few are those who have written with his brilliance of judgement and knowledge. His dignity and absolute sincerity were untainted by envy or ego. Fernau Hall will always be a shining light, a noble man whose words guide and encourage those who love and respect the dance.

Eva Evdokimova
Prima Ballerina Assoluta

Foreword

by Dame Margot Fonteyn

For me Fernau Hall has always been a critic of the highest sensitivity, especially during his many years with the *Daily Telegraph*.

He often displayed great excitement and enthusiasm about the world of dance, and his writings show a depth of understanding based on his own practical experience and the wide knowledge of many forms of dance.

Fernau Hall was a good friend, who took the greatest interest in my unfolding career and the historic development of British ballet through my working with some of the great choreographers like Ashton and MacMillan.

Fernau Hall had a great quality of inspiring and encouraging artists of the dance and for me *The Beauty of Ballet* does much to reflect this wonderful gift.

Dame Margot Fonteyn
Prima Ballerina Assoluta

CHAPTER ONE

Introduction

Ballet, once considered an art with limited appeal, now attracts wider and wider audiences. In its own fashion, it speaks boldly and directly to all manner of people, giving them a special kind of pleasure. One reason for this is that ballet does not depend on words: it appeals straight to the heart with its expressive dance-images, cutting across cultural barriers. A Russian living in Novosibirsk can appreciate *Giselle* just as a deeply as a Dane living in Copenhagen, an American living in San Francisco, or a Chinese inhabitant of Beijing.

Another reason for the constantly rising appeal of ballet is that it brings together a number of arts in such a way that they all contribute strongly to its expressiveness. It is possible to think of ballet as wordless drama, and also as a visual embodiment of music. Being highly pictorial, it can be seen as the coming to life of figures in a setting; and since these dancing figures exist in three dimensions, ballet can be thought of as living sculpture.

To dancers, it is a source of joy, and also of frustration, that their instruments are their own bodies. This means that they can pour themselves totally into their dancing; but they cannot see and assess what they do, and so cannot perfect their dancing without the help of others. Mirrors are essential in any ballet studio, but are of limited use.

A good choreographer (who must be intensely musical) uses music in a subtle, sensitive and creative way. This is essential, for the interaction between music and dancing is fundamental to choreographic expression. The dancer must play the instrument he or she has perfected – a well-trained and well-shaped body – in a musical way, fusing movements and music into dance-images that are strongly projected to the audience.

When we see a great dancer on stage, moving us deeply by the apparently effortless beauty and expressiveness of his or her movements, we see only the tip of the iceberg. Behind every detail of the line of each part of the body (coordinated with the line of other parts of the body), and behind every detail of the timing of the movements in relation to the rhythm and phrasing of the music, there is a great mass of training, extending through all the long years in a ballet school. After joining a company, the dancer works harder than ever in the dance studio: with teachers (for the daily class), with coaches and (if both lucky and talented) with choreographers. A teacher may spend weeks correcting one persistent fault: diagnosing it, tracing it back to its origin, and finding just the right way of correcting it. (Such work requires very rare gifts: great teachers are much harder to find than great dancers.) A coach or choreographer may have to use the utmost imagination and intelligence to put over to a dancer what is needed – using a variety of means, including precise demonstration and spoken phrases likely to strike a spark in the dancer. (Creating the role of the Firebird for Tamara Karsavina, the choreographer Mikhail Fokine told her, 'You are a wild beast – the most dangerous thing faced by any hero of a Russian fairy-tale. And you are oriental: the story of the Firebird came into Russian mythology from Indian mythology.')

Because of the immense richness communicated to eye and ear, ballets could not be written down in a satisfactory way until quite recently,

Giselle, *the mad scene, in a performance by the Bolshoi Ballet, with Alla Mikhalchenko in the title role. Giselle has fallen to the ground, and her mother tries to comfort her.*

Tamara Karsavina in the Fokine ballet The Firebird, *during the pre-war golden age of the Diaghilev Ballets Russes. She wears the magical costume designed by Léon Bakst (1910).*

and therefore had to be transmitted by memory. When a ballet left the repertoire, because of a change of fashion or any other reason, it almost always fell into oblivion. As a result, we have lost a mass of ballets from past centuries, only a handful having survived. In this respect, ballet differs greatly from drama and opera, with their enormous heritage from the past.

This means that much of the history of ballet is really prehistory. We have no access to the actual choreography of almost all the great ballets of the past; we can only do our best to judge their quality, and imagine their styles, from contemporary descriptions, the impact on audiences, visual material such as prints, and the nature and quality of the music. This approach to lost ballets of past centuries has its own fascination, and, like all prehistory, it is very important. Without it, we cannot see, in perspective, those few ballets which do survive from past centuries.

For hundreds of years, during the Middle Ages and the Renaissance, court entertainments involving dancing were staged; the danced interludes took their place alongside singing, instrumental music and elaborate spectacle. But in the 17th century, and in the early years of the 18th, a number of writers suggested that dance and mime could be used in a much more satisfying way if the ancient Graeco-Roman art of pantomime was revived.

Various experiments were carried out, but the major breakthrough happened in London, where theatre managers and artists had greater freedom to try out new ideas than elsewhere. It was John Weaver who, in 1717, staged *The Loves of Mars and Venus* at the Drury Lane Theatre with the outstanding French dancer Louis Dupré and the beautiful English dancer Hester Santlow in the leading parts. Weaver intended his 'dramatick entertainment in dancing' to be a reconstruction of an ancient pantomime described by Lucian of Samosata, but, of course, he had no idea of how this had been danced and mimed, and took the liberty of using a number of dancers instead of just

one. Before tackling his next 'dramatick entertainment', *Orpheus and Eurydice*, Weaver did a great deal of literary research, and no doubt enriched his choreographic vocabulary.

After this breakthrough, there is a clear line of development, with each choreographer standing on the shoulders of his or her predecessors. It was the supremely expressive French dancer, Marie Sallé, who took up the torch from John Weaver: she must have seen *The Loves of Mars and Venus*, since she was dancing in London (as a child prodigy) at the time it was staged, and came of a family of *forains* – travelling entertainers, who were accustomed to seeing everything that could be of use to them.

Like a great many dancers and choreographers of later times, Sallé felt cramped artistically in her home theatre (the Opéra in Paris) and came back to London to create ballets which took London by storm. Such was the power of her choreography and her dancing in the leading role that there were riots in the theatre (with spectators fighting duels) during a gala performance of her first ballet

TOP Grand ballet *ending the court entertainment* Le Ballet des fées des forêts de St Germain *(1625) – danced by French courtiers in rich costumes in 'Roman' style.*
LEFT *Marie Sallé dancing at the Paris Opera, wearing the customary panniers, in an idealized setting. Coloured print after Nicolas Lancret.*

Pygmalion (1734). Wearing a simple muslin tunic instead of the stiff, voluminous costumes then *de rigueur* in Paris, she was able to dance in a free, expressive way, and in her second ballet, *Bacchus et Ariane*, her dancing projected a wide range of emotions, including grief and despair. Such was her expressive musicality that Handel wrote for her the music for yet another ballet, *Terpsicore* – performed as a prologue to his opera *Alcina*. However, at the time Handel was being attacked by supporters of a rival; they howled down *Terpsicore* as well as the opera, and Sallé decided to abandon the idea of continuing her career in London, even though she knew she would be creatively circumscribed at the Opéra.

Back in Paris, while she did manage to insert dramatic *pas de deux*, featuring herself, into operas by Rameau, the costumes (with panniers) were constricting, there were limitations on her developing any of her own ideas, and she retired after five years, even though she was only 33. Even so, she had great influence in Paris. For example, the young Jean-Georges Noverre saw her dancing at royal command performances after her 'retirement', watched her take her daily class in her home, and admired her dancing in the ballets she choreographed for the Opéra Comique at the Foire St. Laurent. Another pioneer choreographer greatly influenced by Sallé was Franz Hilverding from Vienna, who saw her dance in Paris. Her role in the development of ballet is comparable in some ways to that of Monteverdi in the development of opera.

Making his career as *maître de ballet* for the two court theatres in Vienna, Hilverding was supported by a man with rare and extremely important gifts: Count Giacomo Durazzo, director of the court theatres. Here was a creative artistic director who was able to bring together teams of artists and encourage them to extend their artistic range on works of high quality. A contemporary print shows that he commissioned a ballet called *Pygmalion*, which was probably Hilverding's homage to Sallé. Another print shows the last ballet that was choreographed by Hilverding in Vienna: *Le Turc généreux* (1758), watched by Durazzo from a stage box. The joy of this print is that Belotto, the talented artist who created it, suggests the movements of the solo dancers.

Durazzo's supreme achievement as a creative artistic director came in 1761. At this time, he had brought together a superb team – nothing like it was seen until Diaghilev formed his dance company early in the 20th century. Led by Durazzo, all the members of the team united to create *Don Juan*, a ballet with a marvellous harmony between its elements. The librettist Raniero di Calzabigi skilfully adapted Molière's play to the needs of choreography. The German-born composer Gluck was inspired to create a score splendidly suited to a dramatic ballet, with many dramatic changes of tempo, mood and rhythm. Gasparo Angiolini, who had learned the craft of choreography by dancing in Hilverding's ballets, created his own choreography in a style suited to the music and the action.

LEFT Le Turc généreux, *a 'ballet-pantomime' choreographed by Franz Hilverding and performed at a court theatre in Vienna in 1758 for Count Durazzo. Print after Bernardo Bellotto (mis-spelt as Belotti on print).*
OPPOSITE TOP *Gluck's opera* Orphée et Euridice *(Paris version). Choreography by Belinda Quirey, with Marilyn Hill Smith (singer) and Ron Howell (dancer). English Bach Festival, Covent Garden, 1988.*

The 'reform' opera *Orfeo ed Euridice*, produced by the same team a year later, was just as successful as the ballet *Don Juan*, and it still has a place in today's international operatic repertoire. *Don Juan*, on the other hand, fell into obscurity because, although its music score survived, its choreography could not be written down. A reconstruction by the Royal Swedish Ballet, performed at the old Swedish court theatre at Drottningholm, is fascinating to spectators – and television viewers – for a variety of reasons: the theatre dates from the relevant period, and still contains the original machinery for making scene changes; the costumes and scenery are correct in style; and the music is authentic. The Swedish choreographer, Rosina Beck-Friis, and the dancers encountered a number of difficult problems, but made some use of period court dancing (of which much is known), and the production as a whole gives a stimulating impression of what might have been the style of the original ballet.

The dramatic dancing in *Orfeo ed Euridice* (such as the dances of the Furies) is lost beyond recall. However, Belinda Quirey, after working for half a century in London on the reconstitution of the noble court dances of the baroque era (drawing on dance notation, descriptions and a study of the evolution of baroque out of Renaissance dancing) was able, in the English Bach Society's 1988 production of the French version of the Gluck opera at Covent Garden, to bring together three of the best dancers trained by her in a superb 'minuet of the Blessed Spirits'. Here was the authentic rise and fall of the bodies, the correspondingly elegant and fluid movements of the hands and arms, and patterns curving over the space of the stage in the baroque style, all closely and sensitively matched to Gluck's music, and taking spectators back to the noble court dancing that flourished before (and during) the rise of the new type of ballet – the *ballet d'action*.

The second ballet created by Durazzo's team, *Semiramide* (1765), based on a tragedy by Voltaire, had in its principal role Mlle. Nancy, who had been trained by Noverre in Stuttgart. She danced so expressively that the audience trembled and wept.

Noverre's long career as a choreographer overlapped those of Hilverding and Angiolini. He and Angiolini were rivals, battling against each other in published *Letters* and prefaces to ballets in which each claimed priority for the new ideas. Noverre was a brilliant writer, widely read by those who advocated *ballets d'action*, and the *Letters* he had published in Stuttgart, Lyons and Paris – giving a clear idea of his balletic ideals and his criticisms of established fashions – had great influence on other choreographers, right up to the present day. Angiolini lacked Noverre's brilliance as a writer, so he was happy to let Calzabigi write his *Letters* and prefaces to programmes.

Noverre might well have put his ideas into

Jason et Medée, *with choreography by Noverre (usual title* Medée et Jason*). Creusa (Giovanna Bacelli) and Jason (Gaetan Vestris) confront Medea (Adelaide Simonet). The poses suggest Noverre's forceful mime.*

practice much earlier had he been able to pursue his career in London, following in the footsteps of Sallé, for there he would have had artistic freedom (under the aegis of the great actor David Garrick, who brought him to London in 1755, and whose acting greatly influenced him). But the outbreak of war between France and England in 1756 made it necessary for Noverre to leave London – much to Garrick's regret and his own.

Fortunately for Noverre, Duke Carl Eugen of Württemberg had become accustomed to spend lavishly on court entertainments in Stuttgart, using the money gained by hiring out his soldiers to foreign potentates – notably the king of France – and he invited Noverre to come to Stuttgart. There Noverre was able to develop to full maturity, choreographing a series of remarkable tragic ballets in collaboration with various talented composers, the outstanding scenic designer Servandoni, and the equally remarkable costume designer Boquet; what is more, he had at his disposal twenty of the finest French solo dancers of the day, including Vestris, Le Picq and Dauberval (who started his career as a choreographer while working with Noverre). Noverre also had a *corps de ballet* of 100, and made good use of them. Such was the intensity of feeling projected in Noverre's ballet *Medée et Jason* that some women fainted when it was first performed. Paris had fine teachers who constantly enlarged and perfected the ballet technique and produced a number of fine dancers; but it was imaginative choreographers such as Noverre and Angiolini, working away from Paris, who induced the dancers to use their technical skill as a support for choreographic expression.

After a few years, Duke Carl Eugen exhausted the Württemberg treasury, and he was persuaded by his mistress to cut down his expenditure on the theatre. Then Durazzo, deprived of the services of Angiolini (who had left for St Petersburg) brought Noverre to Vienna. The Count once again demonstrated the imagination and good judgement characteristic of him by permitting Noverre to bring a number of dancers with him, including some trained by him. Noverre used a wide variety of themes in Stuttgart and Vienna. *Les Amours de Henri IV*, for example, was based on the life of one of France's greatest kings (a Huguenot who cheerfully became a nominal Catholic when he realized that a king of France could not be a Protestant). In *Antoine et Cléopâtre*, he put to good use his admiration for Shakespeare, gained during his early stay in London. Other ballets were based on Greek myths.

Noverre ended his creative career in London, which he made the centre of the ballet world in the

closing years of the 18th century. His ballets were immensely popular with London audiences, not least because Noverre, as usual, brought together an outstanding group of dancers – including two men who were to become outstanding choreographers, Charles-Louis Didelot and Salvatore Viganò.

After Noverre's retirement, Didelot created a series of fine ballets in London, maintaining this city as the creative capital of the ballet world. His most successful London ballet, *Flore et Zéphyre*, was charmingly Anacreontic; he took it with him when he returned to St Petersburg in 1816, where it survived in the repertoire right up to the 20th century. Didelot first went to St Petersburg in 1801, making the city a great centre of ballet, training a large number of fine dancers, and staging a number of new ballets – owing much to Noverre, but avoiding Noverre's propensity for stressing mime at the expense of expressive dancing. (When Didelot staged Noverre's most famous ballet *Medée et Jason* in Russia, he modified the choreography somewhat.)

One of the finest ballets he created there was *Raoul de Créquis*, or *The Return from the Crusades* (using a theme already tackled by his great contemporary in Milan, Viganò). Here Didelot developed a number of striking dramatic effects and bold characterizations, while showing his own musicality and demanding musicality from his dancers, and freely alternating between tragedy and comedy in a way characteristic of him. Having a great love of oriental dances, he tackled an Eastern theme in another remarkable ballet: *The Prisoner of the Caucasus*, based on a poem by Pushkin. Istomina, a great Russian dancer, came to maturity dancing a wide variety of roles in Didelot's ballets, and created an unforgettable impression as the Circassian Girl in *The Prisoner of the Caucasus*. Pushkin immortalized Istomina in his poem *Eugene Onegin*, and wrote of Didelot that he was 'winged by fame'.

Like Didelot, Salvatore Viganò – the other supreme choreographer of the early decades of the 19th century – came under the direct influence of Noverre while dancing in the latter's ballet in London; later, he dominated ballet in Milan just as Didelot did in St Petersburg. Intensely original and imaginative – Stendhal called him the 'Shakespeare of ballet' – he created expressive dance-images which broke down the familiar division between dancing and mime. Being rich, he was able to take as long as he liked to stage his ballets at La Scala, working out every nuance of movement and grouping with the utmost care. Himself a master of every aspect of the theatre, he had no need of a Durazzo: his ballets were total works of art, with magnificent designs by the great Alessandro Sanquirico, and music carefully assembled by himself – to match his choreographic ideas – from the works of a number of composers, or else self-composed.

Being a fine musician, Viganò took as much care over the music of his ballets as he did over the other elements – indeed, he commissioned the music for *The Creatures of Prometheus* from Beethoven – and this music helps us to form some idea of his style as a choreographer.

He tackled a splendid variety of subjects: a rebellion in Russia against Peter the Great (*Gli Strelizzi*), Greek myths (*Dedalo e Icare, I Titani*), a play by Shakespeare (*Otello*), the story of a French martyr-saint (*Giovanna d'Arco*) and so on.

Viganò, together with Didelot and their predecessors, firmly established ballet as a major theatrical art.

The Didelot ballet Flore et Zéphyre, *reconstructed by Mary Skeaping and performed at the Drottningholm court theatre, with dancers of the Royal Swedish Ballet.*

CHAPTER TWO

'La Fille mal gardée'

Regrettably, all the masterpieces of Didelot and Viganò, so admired in their day, have fallen into oblivion. Very fortunately, however, an earlier ballet by Dauberval, created by him in Bordeaux in 1789, has been preserved with at least part of the original choreographic text – and with changes by sensitive choreographers who showed a real understanding of Dauberval's style. With *La Fille mal gardée* we move from prehistory into history.

Dauberval could never have created this masterpiece – in the genre of artless, real-life comedy that he himself invented – at the Paris Opéra, where he was hemmed in by the usual intrigues. After retiring in despair from the Opéra, he returned to Bordeaux, where he became the first resident *maître de ballet* of the magnificent Grand-Théâtre (the finest in France), and turned the city into a major centre of ballet.

La Fille mal gardée (*The Unguarded Daughter*) was inspired by a painting by P.A. Baudouin showing a mother in a barn, upbraiding her daughter – who has clearly been making love to a man who is running away, up a flight of steps. Dauberval saw an engraving of this painting in the window of a shop in Bordeaux, and for some time he thought about creating a ballet based on this print. In 1789, he was able to stage it at the Grand-Théâtre, with his wife – the talented dancer Mlle.

Théodore – as the heroine Lise. At this point in French history the ballet was highly acceptable, swept as France was by new ideas of social change, and Dauberval's choreography – set to charming music, probably arranged by himself from French folk tunes – had a new kind of magic.

Very soon, the ballet was staged by Dauberval with great success in London, in Venice by Viganò, and possibly even in faraway Philadelphia before the end of the 18th century. In fact, it became the most widely performed of any ballet. Composers revised the music: when the ballet was staged by Jean Aumer at the Paris Opéra in 1828, Louis-Joseph Ferdinand Hérold added some of his own compositions, as well as two passages from Rossini operas, while Paul Taglioni used a new score by Peter Ludwig Hertel when he staged it in Berlin in 1864.

remarkable talents of the Italian ballerina Virginia Zucchi. Among other things, Ivanov had Zucchi wear blocked shoes and use the full *pointe* instead of the half-*pointe* of the original choreography. (*Pointe*-work came into existence after Dauberval created the ballet.) Ivanov and Zucchi both did wonders, showing respect for the original choreography but giving it new vitality, and the ballet became even more popular than before: it remained the most popular of all ballets in St. Petersburg. Ivanov used the Hertel music, but the traditional Russian version of the ballet that has come down to us (with its Dauberval choreography, revised by Didelot and Ivanov) has such a strong period flavour that we can be certain that, through it, we make a direct (and precious) contact with a masterpiece created in the 18th century.

LEFT La Fille mal gardée, *with new choreography by Frederick Ashton for the Royal Ballet, 1960. The scene in the fields: David Wall as Colas, Wendy Ellis as Lise, c. 1980.*
RIGHT La Fille mal gardée, *produced by Alexander Gorsky for Bolshoi Ballet, Moscow, c. 1920. Lise and Colin (as Russians call Colas) have been discovered in a compromising situation.*

Crucial to the survival of this ballet, with much of Dauberval's original choreography, was its production in St. Petersburg in 1827 by Didelot, who had been taught the role of Colas by Dauberval himself. Since Didelot was a highly gifted choreographer, it is possible that he made some changes to the choreography, while respecting Dauberval's style.

The ballet remained a great favourite in Russia, but technically it was much less challenging than later ballets such as *Giselle*. In 1885, Marius Petipa gave his assistant Lev Ivanov – the first great Russian choreographer – the task of revising the central female role so that it made fuller use of the

Many new versions were created in the 20th century – notably a much revised and much condensed one by Bronislava Nijinska, preserved in the repertoire of American Ballet Theater. The Dauberval/Didelot/Ivanov version was preserved by one of the finest artists ever to interpret Lise, Aleksandra Balashova – who was so good in the role in the early years of this century that she was sometimes invited to come from the Bolshoi in Moscow to dance the role at the Maryinsky in St. Petersburg (a great honour for her). She also staged a number of excellent productions of the ballet in Paris and elsewhere.

As Balashova – the main repository of the

The first scene of Ashton's version for the Royal Ballet of La Fille mal gardée, *with Alexander Grant (at right) as the half-witted Alain.*

traditional Franco-Russian choreography (and especially that of Lise, her favourite role) – got older, it became more and more likely that the traditional *La Fille mal gardée* would be lost, as ballet masters in the Soviet Union began to make more and destructive changes in almost all old ballets. The danger was acute, for Balashova had been born as early as 1887. Because of this, Rudolf Benesh, founder/director of the Institute of Choreology in London, arranged for the choreologist Monica Parker (later to become director of the Institute) to go to Ljubljana in Yugoslavia in 1969 to record what turned out to be Balashova's last production; then Balashova and the French soloist who was dancing Lise were brought to London so that Monica Parker could check her choreographic score.

Something very strange – almost a miracle – happened when Frederick Ashton staged his own version for the Royal Ballet in 1960. He was very fortunate in having the advice and help of Tamara Karsavina, who had been superb as Lise in the traditional Franco-Russian version at the pre-Revolution Maryinsky, and remembered the whole ballet well. Guided by her, he created a new ballet which turned out to be one of his finest, showing all his talents to perfection, and suggesting that one part of him really belonged to the 18th century. What is more, he had Karsavina revive the famous mime scene, which occurs soon after the beginning of Act II, in which Lise imagines herself getting married and bringing up children. Such was Ashton's feeling for style that this scene does not stand out as foreign to the rest of his ballet: the traditional choreography (adapted to Hérold's music) blends perfectly into Ashton's choreography.

Ashton's *Fille* took its place in the Royal Ballet's repertoire alongside such established classics as *Giselle* and *Swan Lake*. Numerous remarkable ballerinas, such as Nadia Nerina (who created the Ashton version of Lise), Svetlana Beriosova and Merle Park, did wonders with the role of the heroine – following in the footsteps of Zucchi, Kshessinskaya, Preobrazhenskaya, Karsavina and Balashova – and interpretations of the other leading roles have been no less satisfying, with Ashton taking care with the casting and giving a final polish to the dancing at each revival.

CHAPTER THREE

The Romantic Ballet

Romanticism arose as an expression of a period of violent change: social and political changes which flowered in the turmoil of the French Revolution, the wars of Napoleon and the Industrial Revolution which began in England. It emerged first in German and English literature, and soon dominated painting and music. It came to ballet last of all, but made such a profound impact that it continued to shape ballet right up to the first decade of the 20th century. Indeed, choreographers are still creating ballets which may properly be called romantic.

Romantic artists were fascinated by anything that was mysterious, exotic, supernatural, unattainable, remote in time, or dream-like. Emotion was glorified at the expense of form and control – and yet the best writers, painters, composers and choreographers showed a superb understanding of the importance of these two elements as they tackled their new themes.

Being a synthesis of many arts, ballet was able to incarnate the spirit of romanticism superbly. Romantic choreographers profited by the fact that dancers had learned to suggest mysterious immateriality and the supernatural by high, floating leaps and by balancing on the tip of a toe – thus implying that they were weightless, unaffected by gravity as mere mortals are. Fresh opportunities for expressive dancing by ballerinas were thus opened up, and a number of supreme cosmopolitan ballerinas emerged and were idolized by the public. Female dancing became accepted as the most perfect expression of the romantic spirit; male dancing could not compete, and so rapidly decayed (although the great romantic choreographers Jules Perrot and August Bournonville – both of whom were fine dancers – took care to preserve it in their ballets).

Marie Taglioni, the first of the romantic superstars, was typical of these artists in that her aura of mysterious immateriality was based on a very strong technique – all these dancers were superb in deploying the art that conceals art. She took the title role in the pioneering romantic

Marie Taglioni in the title role of the original version of La Sylphide *(1832), with choreography by Filippo Taglioni. Lithograph after A.E. Chalon.*

ballet, *La Sylphide* (1832), with choreography by her father, Filippo Taglioni. Wearing a long, flimsy white skirt that did not impede her movements, leaping high with marvellous grace and lightness, and occasionally posing on the tip of her toe – a pose which could not last long, unless she was supported by her partner, because her shoes were unblocked – she seemed the embodiment of the supernatural creature of the forest glades whom James, the young Scotsman, sees in a dream, and the embodiment of his hidden desires. She bewitches him, and he abandons his bride to follow her into the forest – with tragic results.

La Sylphide was an overwhelming success, and changed the face of ballet: its influence on subsequent ballets was so powerful that it can still be felt today. Not that Filippo Taglioni was a great choreographer, but he had the good sense to do the right thing at the right time with the right ballerina, his daughter Marie – who had been very carefully trained by him.

By good fortune, one of the two finest choreographers of the day, August Bournonville, came from Copenhagen to Paris in 1834 with his finest pupil, Lucile Grahn, then aged 15. He saw *La Sylphide*, realized at once its significance – among other things, he saw it would provide Grahn with an ideal role – and decided to stage his version of the ballet (*Sylfiden*) in Copenhagen.

The trouble was that the charge for the rights in Jean Schneitzhoeffer's music was more than the Danes could afford, so Bournonville commissioned a new score from the Norwegian composer Baron Herman Severin von Løvenskjold, keeping the original libretto. Løvenskjold, having far more talent than Schneitzhoeffer, provided Bournonville with a charming score containing appropriately delicate melodies for the Sylphide, stirring Scottish dances, and ferocious music for the Witch – thus helping Bournonville to improve on Filippo Taglioni. Being a fine dancer, and strongly resistent to the fashionable denigration of male dancing as unsuitable for Romantic ballet, Bournonville took care to build up the role of the hero James for himself; and he was inspired by Lucile Grahn (with whom he was in love) to create a role combining mystery, charm and humour, exactly attuned to the rare qualities of the young ballerina.

The result was a masterpiece; and because the Danes had (and have) the greatest respect for Bournonville, this ballet has been preserved as part of the Bournonville repertoire, which has remained the pride and joy of the Royal Danish Ballet. It is now performed by a good many companies around the world, but dancers must be trained in the Bournonville 'school' if they are to bring out all its qualities – and the ballerina taking the role of the Sylphide must be something very special. (The Bournonville 'school' differs somewhat from the old French 'school' partly because Bournonville adapted the old French 'school' to his own dancing: he was good at beaten steps and leaps, but less good at pirouettes.)

Poor Bournonville: Grahn was not interested in marrying him, and left Denmark to become one of the five cosmopolitan superstars of the Romantic Ballet. The others were Marie Taglioni (Italian-Swedish), Carlotta Grisi (Italian), Fanny Elssler (Austrian) and Fanny Cerrito (Italian). Each of these great artists had a striking personality and a style all her own, so that they gave very different interpretations to the central roles of the ballets of the day – much to the delight of audiences.

Bournonville had a long career and created a number of other fine ballets in Copenhagen, some of which have been preserved. However, it was the special magic that he gave to his choreography for his beloved Grahn that has caused this ballet to stand alongside Jules Perrot's *Giselle* as one of the two surviving supreme masterpieces of Romantic ballet.

Because Bournonville committed a gross error of *lèse-majesté* by publicly addressing the king of Denmark at a performance in the Royal Theatre in Copenhagen, he had to leave Denmark for six months. During this enforced holiday, he visited a number of European cities, but it was Naples which made the most vivid impression on him. He observed very carefully the exuberant street life there, and incorporated his observations, after his return to Copenhagen, into one of the most popular of all his ballets, *Napoli* – full of striking characters, expressive Neapolitan gestures and, in the last act, light-hearted Italianate dances. (Following tradition, these are watched by the children of the Royal Danish Ballet School, standing on a bridge at the back of the stage.) Later ballets evoked the atmosphere of a number of other countries. *Kermesse at Bruges*, for example, evokes Flanders in the 17th century, and weaves a number of sparkling dances into a legend of three brothers and a magic violin. *A Folk Tale* also presents an ancient legend, with a scene in the subterranean hall of the Troll Woman, and two very grotesque brothers, Diderik and Viderik. All these ballets have happily survived, together with others in lighter vein.

The Royal Danish Ballet has also preserved a suite of *divertissements* – *The Caprices of Cupid and the Ballet Master* – which date from the same year as *La Fille mal gardée*: 1786. Its choreographer, Vincenzo Galeotti, was much influenced by Noverre and Angiolini, and created a long series of ambitious *ballets d'action* in Copenhagen; but Bournonville dropped all but *The Caprices* from the repertoire, claiming that Galeotti's serious ballets had lost their appeal to the public.

Bournonville and Jules Perrot were friends; they had been fellow-students of the great French teacher Auguste Vestris a few years earlier, and when Bournonville paid tribute to this teacher by depicting a Vestris class in Act I of his ballet *Konservatoriet*, he included some male solos choreographed by his friend Perrot.

The latter, too, created a number of fine ballets, being much influenced by the *Letters* of Noverre.

OPPOSITE *Opening pose of* Le Pas de quatre, *choreographed by Jules Perrot in London in 1845. (L to r) Carlotta Grisi, Marie Taglioni, Lucile Grahn, Fanny Cerrito. Lithograph after A.E. Chalon.*
RIGHT *Carlotta Grisi in the title role of* Giselle *(Act II). Lithograph by John Brandard.*

The last act of Bournonville's Napoli. *Young dancers watch from the bridge – thus absorbing the Bournonville style, as young Danish dancers have done since 1842. Scottish Ballet, 1986.*

Regrettably, only one of Perrot's ballets has survived, having been preserved by the Imperial Russian Ballet in St Petersburg, but it *is* his masterpiece, *Giselle*. Just as Bournonville created *La Sylphide* for his beloved Lucile Grahn, Perrot devised the role of Giselle for his beloved Carlotta Grisi – and he created a splendid male role for her partner in the ballet (Count Albrecht). Like Bournonville, he was determined to preserve traditions of male dancing – and he knew that he would be able to dance this role himself once he took the ballet away from Paris. At the Paris Opéra he created the main part of the choreography – the roles of Giselle and Albrecht – but he was in disfavour because he had left the Opéra, so Jean Coralli choreographed the other parts and was given all the credit. Once Perrot was in command, in London and St Petersburg, he was able to rework the whole of the ballet to his satisfaction.

What is unique about *Giselle*, among all the ballets created at this time, is that the ballerina has the great challenge of presenting the heroine in three different aspects. For most of Act I, she is an innocent village maiden, deeply in love with 'Loys', her simple peasant lover who is actually the nobleman Albrecht. Towards the end of the act, when she discovers Loys' true identity and that he is already betrothed, she has a powerful mad scene, ending in her death. And in Act II, she is one of the ghost-like Wilis (girls who have died before their wedding nights because of the faithlessness of their lovers), subject to the commands of the dreaded Queen of the Wilis (a splendidly dramatic role), but still retaining her profound love for Albrecht and determined to protect him.

With *Giselle*, Perrot was fortunate in having at his disposal music that was of much better quality than the usual hack music generally commissioned for ballet at this time. Adolphe Adam's music may not be as remarkable as that of his intensely Romantic contemporaries Chopin, Berlioz and Schumann, but it is good enough to stand up to being heard hundreds of times, and it suits the action superbly. One of Adam's best ideas was to give Giselle a *leitmotif* – which Perrot was able to use in a highly imaginative way. Early in the ballet, we see Giselle and Albrecht performing an *enchaînement – ballotté, ballotté, ballonné, coupé-jeté* – to Giselle's *leitmotif*; these are standard classroom steps, but linked to the music so imaginatively by Perrot that they express Giselle's simple, trusting nature and her love for Albrecht. In the mad scene, Giselle performs this *enchaînement* again, just before her death, in a way which evokes her madness: she 'marks' the steps instead of performing them properly (so that they are almost unrecognizable), and includes them at the end of a strange and frightening sequence in which she runs through disconnected fragments of all the dancing and mime she had done before she had found herself betrayed. In Act II, Perrot takes us into a world of moonlight and mystery; now the choreography is more complex and fluid, breaking away from the classroom with imaginative movements of the arms, and showing a poetic quality related to the poetry of Heine (who discovered the legend of the Wilis) and Gautier (who proposed a ballet based on this legend).

One of the many delights of *Giselle* is the opportunity it offers to the ballerina to develop her own interpretation. This was true even while Perrot, working in London, was still closely associated with his ballet. Grisi, who created the title role, projected a Giselle who was essentially lyrical, whereas Elssler – a strong, dramatic dancer – stressed the emotional aspects, and gave such power to the mad scene that traces of her interpretation are likely to emerge when any subsequent ballerina comes to interpret it. Indeed, the survival of the ballet is due to the fact that it offers such a challenge to the artist tackling Giselle. Outside Russia, the ballet fell into obscurity in the 1850s, but in Russia, the ballerinas so enjoyed attempting this role, with the diverse opportunities it offered them in its two sharply contrasted acts, that they fought successfully every attempt to drop it.

Benjamin Lumley, director of Her Majesty's Theatre in London (where Perrot worked from 1842 to 1848) asked the choreographer to create – as a publicity stunt – a ballet bringing together four of the superstars of the day: Taglioni, Grisi, Grahn and Cerrito. Perrot tackled *Le Pas de quatre* with assured professionalism, giving each

Galina Ulanova, after coaching Ekaterina Maximova as Giselle, adjusts her make-up before her remarkable debut in this role with the Bolshoi Ballet.

dancer *enchaînements* of the type she did best. The result was a sensation: never before had these stars danced together. In 1936, Keith Lester devised an intelligent reconstruction of this ballet for the Markova–Dolin Ballet, taking account of descriptions of the way each star danced; regrettably, this reconstruction has been replaced by one devised by Anton Dolin which virtually ignores the differing styles of the original artists.

Perrot was ballet master in St Petersburg from 1848 to 1859 – restaging his best ballets, creating new ones, and maintaining the art of ballet at a high level while it was declining everywhere else except in Denmark. Unfortunately, this intensely musical choreographer usually had to use conventional music, by Cesare Pugni and other second-rate composers, which gave him little chance to show his extraordinary talent at full stretch, as he had in *Giselle*.

Giselle, *Act II, as performed by the Kirov Ballet in Paris, with Ekaterina Maximova (Giselle) and Vladimir Vasiliev (Albrecht) appearing as guest artists.*

CHAPTER FOUR

'Coppélia'

Except in Russia and Denmark, the art of ballet decayed seriously in the second half of the 19th century. Indeed, people forgot that it ever had been a great art, regarding it only as light entertainment. Male dancing almost disappeared, and ballerinas were regarded as rather glamorous prostitutes or courtesans.

In 1870, however, there was a remarkable (though very brief) recovery in Paris, brought about by the efforts of a group of gifted and intelligent people with minds of their own.

The project for *Coppélia* was originated by Charles-Louis-Etienne Nuitter, who had written the librettos of a number of Offenbach operettas, and some ballets. He recognized the fine possibilities for ballet contained in E.T.A. Hoffmann's story 'Der Sandmann' and invented a heroine, Swanilda, who tests her sweetheart Franz's love by pretending to be Coppélia, the life-like wax doll that its maker Dr Coppelius tries to animate with magic – for Nuitter understood that the romantic horrors of the original story would need to be watered down. He also realized how well suited the role of the doll coming to life would be to the

OPPOSITE BELOW *Coppélia (Russian version), as performed by London Festival Ballet, with Peter Schaufuss as Franz and Lucia Truglia as Swanilda.*
RIGHT *Merle Park – intensely musical, and coached by Maria Fay – makes an individual and compelling debut as Swanilda in the Royal Ballet's* Coppélia. *Stanley Holden portrays an amusing Dr Coppelius (1964).*

superb talents of the highly intelligent young French *danseuse* Léontine Beaugrand, with a central role given to a charming soubrette. The talented choreographer Arthur Saint-Léon – a close friend of Nuitter, and well aware of Beaugrand's abilities – was fascinated by the project, and helped Nuitter to shape it, suggesting the inclusion of an adapted version of a *csardas*, a Hungarian folk dance. The young composer Léo Delibes had already made his mark in ballet with his score for *La Source*, and had just the right talent for a comedy ballet with a soubrette in the central role.

The management of the Paris Opéra approved the project, Delibes wrote his delectable music, and Saint-Léon began rehearsals, with Beaugrand doing wonders with the leading role of Swanilda. The role of Franz was taken by a *danseuse en travesti*, Eugénie Fiocre, as was the custom in Paris at this time. (Male dancing had almost disappeared in Paris; it was of no interest to the balletomanes.) Then Perrin – the keen businessman who directed the Opéra – decided he would make more money with a guest artist from abroad, and brought in the 16-year-old Italian dancer Giuseppina Bozacchi.

The ballet had such quality that it was a success even though it suffered from the absence of Beaugrand, ideal for Swanilda. After Bozacchi died of fever on her 17th birthday during the seige of Paris, Beaugrand triumphed in the role, being witty, intelligent, roguish, vivacious and teasing in a very French way. (In private life, she was known as a wit.)

Because of its popularity, this ballet acquired a permanent place in the repertoire – notwithstanding changes in fashion. Indeed, most of the choreography survived well into the 20th century at the Opéra. In 1967, Peter Brinson, director of the Royal Ballet's travelling group 'Ballet for All', asked Paulette Dynalix – an *étoile* of the Opéra and famous for her interpretation of the *travesti* role of Franz – to reconstruct what survived of the ballet (the first two acts) for his ballet-play *Two Coppélias*. Dynalix performed this task admirably, and showed how wrong it had been for the Opéra to scrap it. Yvonne Cartier, a highly intelligent and versatile dancer, was delightful as Franz; coached by Dynalix, she was masculine in a stylized, charmingly androgynous way.

The Russian version, which Petipa commissioned from Lev Ivanov in 1884, was a landmark in ballet history, for it gave this great choreographer his first chance to show his sense of style, musicality and many other qualities in a complete ballet. Throughout his *Coppélia*, he did wonders with the Delibes music, and created choreography which clearly established the personalities and moods of the main characters: Swanilda, Franz and Dr Coppelius (a mime role).

Generations of ballerinas have entranced audiences with their interpretations of the Franco-Russian Swanilda, who must tease Dr Coppelius, but not be too cruel. Swanilda must be danced by an artist with a flair for *demi-caractère* roles. She symbolizes youth and reality, whereas Dr Coppelius symbolizes the eccentric artist who lives in a dream world; he really believes that he has created a doll which he can bring to life. He is devastated when his dream is destroyed by Swanilda, and that is why at first he angrily rejects the purse of money with which she tries to placate him. Though this is a comedy ballet, it has a serious theme, and fine artists, understanding this, bring out both the comedy and the sad undercurrents.

CHAPTER FIVE

Petipa

We owe a great debt of gratitude to the French choreographer Marius Petipa, for he kept the art of ballet alive in Russia for half a century, during a period of decadence elsewhere. During that time he created at least one full-length ballet each year, as well as smaller pieces. Few have survived, for they were constructed according to a strict formula and did not differ much from each other; but despite these faults, they ensured that interest in ballet never disappeared in St. Petersburg.

Whatever the place, period or theme, Petipa gave the dancers much the same patterns of steps. The music from the staff composers of the Imperial Ballet in St. Petersburg was also much the same for each ballet: bright, ephemeral suites of bouncy waltzes, marches and so on. The designers produced conventional settings and costumes, taking little account of the place or period in which the ballet was set.

If a ballerina liked a variation that Petipa had created for her, she could transfer it into another role, even though this one might, in theory, be quite different. Such behaviour did not bother Petipa: if he revived a ballet with a different ballerina in the principal role, he was happy to change the choreography to give her the steps she liked. Petipa took over and greatly stressed a number of standard formulas: a *pas de deux*, for example, always took the form of an *entrée* and *adagio* for both dancers, male dancer's variation, ballerina's variation, and *coda* for both dancers. Such *pas de deux* were almost always showpieces, displays of virtuosity; they were interchangeable, and any of them could be lifted out of the ballet and performed on its own. (A number of them are performed in gala programmes nowadays.)

Petipa greatly admired Perrot, but knew better than to try to create ballets like his. When

Bournonville, visiting Russia in 1874, asked Petipa why he stuffed his ballets with *divertissements*, Petipa told him that that was what was required of him.

In fact, Petipa did have real talent – as he showed when he choreographed Act IV of *La Bayadère* – the 'Kingdom of the Shades'. This act became greatly prized in Russia because it represented the first sign of a revival of Romanticism. It began with a line of *danseuses* from the *corps de ballet* slowly descending a ramp, making a long series of *arabesques penchées*, with the torso bending forward deeply. The 'Kingdom of the Shades' act is now performed in many countries on its own.

Petipa was accustomed to order music from the staff composers as if he were ordering furniture, for they were incapable of writing music of quality. However, after the appointment of Ivan Vsevolozhky as director of the Imperial Theatres, excellent music was used: he abolished the institution of staff composers in 1886, and demanded the staging of a version of *Coppélia*, with its music by Delibes. Vsevolozhky took another major step forward when he commissioned Pyotr Tchaikovsky to write the music for *The Sleeping Beauty*. Petipa realized that, at last, he could make exacting demands on a composer, and he worked out in detail his requirements – which Tchaikovsky was delighted to follow. The result was Petipa's masterpiece. One might object that it has far too many *divertissements* and processions; but that was what audiences required of Petipa, and

Petipa's The Sleeping Beauty, *as performed by the Royal Ballet at Covent Garden.*

LEFT *Petipa's* La Bayadère, *Act IV, 'The Kingdom of the Shades'. Royal Ballet at Covent Garden, 1982.*
RIGHT *Margot Fonteyn (Odette) and Michael Somes (Prince Siegfried) in the* pas de deux *in* Swan Lake, *Act II. Sadler's Wells Ballet at Covent Garden, 1953.*

he was inspired by Tchaikovsky's music to create dances showing musicality, lightness and variety. Every ballerina feels she must face the challenge of the title role, for it gives her a splendid chance to show her skill and artistry. The role is a tough one, however, for she must launch out on the very difficult Rose Adagio in Act I – with four different partners – soon after her first entrance, and follow her first sequence of balances with an even more difficult sequence. The variation which follows is a jewel: the steps have a delicacy which matches the delicacy of Tchaikovsky's music.

For some reason, when Petipa came to do *Swan Lake* four years later in 1894, he choreographed Act I in a pedestrian fashion. However, when he reached the end of Act III and the *pas de deux* of Odile (the daughter of the evil magician Von Rotbart) and Prince Siegfried (who has fallen in love with Odette, transformed into the queen of the swans by the magician), he showed mastery, having Odile repeat some of the magical dance-images created by Ivanov in Act II, thus putting Prince Siegfried under a spell, and convincing him that Odile really is his beloved swan queen. (This *pas de deux* is so different from anything else in Petipa's *oeuvre* that he may well have assigned it to Ivanov – something he was inclined to do.)

Petipa, always prepared to do anything to please his superiors and the public, took the advantage of the fact that the role of Odette–Odile was created for the Italian ballerina Pierina Legnani – a dazzling virtuoso as well as a gifted artist – and assigned to her in the coda the most dazzling of all the feats of virtuosity brought to Russia by the Italian stars: 32 *fouettés*. This feat – involving the dancer turning on one leg while the other whips out to the side and to the knee, 32 times in quick succession – has little to do with the role, and represents a fearful if not impossible challenge to those ballerinas who have all the gifts needed to interpret both Odette and her wicked imposter Odile, but are by their physique unsuited to the *fouettés*.

Three years after the staging of *Beauty*, Tchaikovsky died, and Petipa turned to another gifted composer, Alexander Glazunov. Only one of his Glazunov ballets, *Raymonda*, has won a permanent place in the repertoire; but even in this, there is little action in the first two acts. In fact, outside the Soviet Union, the last act, which includes the Hungarian dances that form part of the wedding celebrations of Raymonda and her Crusader lover Jean de Brienne, is usually performed on its own. Here there is a delightful interweaving of dances for the soloists and groups of various sizes, and Petipa showed himself at his most deft and beguiling in the Hungarian solo, in which Raymonda uses Hungarian arm positions combined with elegant *pointe*-work.

The big pas de deux *in Act II of* Swan Lake, *choreography by Ivanov, with Nina Timofeyeva as Odette. Bolshoi Ballet, 1963.*

CHAPTER SIX

Ivanov

Lev Ivanov, the first truly great Russian choreographer, had a difficult time under Petipa. Extremely musical – Ivanov played the piano superbly – he was able to create choreography that moved through the music in a highly expressive way, respecting the shape of the music, yet establishing its own clear-cut imagery, complementing the music rather than following it. To give full justice to a dance-image created by Ivanov when working at the peak of his ability, dancers must sing the music to themselves rather than counting the beats (as they may do in a Petipa ballet). However, Petipa hardly ever gave Ivanov a chance to work on his own – he laid out the structure of all the ballets, occasionally using Ivanov's choreography but taking the credit. Easy-going Ivanov never protested, even though in his heart he must have known that his talents far exceeded those of his domineering superior.

Ivanov had much more of a free hand than usual when, in 1890, Petipa assigned to him the Polovtsian Dances in the opera *Prince Igor*. The Borodin music showed clear oriental influences – music which gave Ivanov a chance to show his supreme musicality. Diaghilev knew very well what he was doing when he asked Fokine to create a revised version of these dances for the first season of his Ballets Russes in Paris in 1909: although they were quite unlike those of the Kipchak Tartars (the real Polovtsi), they had a splendidly wild exoticism which matched the ferocity of Borodin's music, and the Parisian

The Nutcracker, with choreography by Ivanov. 'The Dance of the Snowflakes', with 'snow' falling on the dancers. Royal Ballet at Covent Garden, 1985.

audience adored them. In fact, what they saw was quite close to Ivanov's originals. In Russia, the Fokine version remained unknown: it was Ivanov's choreography which was preserved – and this shows that, long before the breath-taking Paris season of 1909, Ivanov had been an artist of extraordinary originality and versatility, as much at home in the lighthearted, very Parisian 'Silesia' of *Coppélia* as on the steppes of Central Asia.

Ivanov's next major assignment came in 1892, but unfortunately this production was heartbreakingly unworthy of the giant talents of Tchaikovsky and Ivanov. In that year, both of these great artists were given the task of working on *The Nutcracker*, and thanks to the combined efforts of Vsevolozhsky and Petipa, Tchaikovsky and Ivanov were faced with a libretto which could only result in a very unsatisfactory ballet: the ballerina who should be the centrepiece (the Sugar Plum Fairy) only appears in Act II to dance one *pas de deux*; the action in Act I – building up to the battle of the mice and the toy soldiers – is very feeble; and so on. When Vsevolozhsky chose this story, he showed poor judgement; and when Tchaikovsky received the detailed plans he was appalled. Being a great composer, he still managed to write attractive music, but he worked at far below his best level, except in certain dances such as the variation of the Sugar Plum Fairy.

LEFT *Polovtsian dances from* Prince Igor, *as adapted by Fokine from Ivanov's original choreography for the opera. London Festival Ballet, 1979.*

Ivanov was just as dismayed as Tchaikovsky, and could make little of Petipa's libretto. Some of his extraordinary talent did emerge in the *corps de ballet*'s Dance of the Snowflakes, with its swirling masses of *danseuses* suggesting the whirling of snowflakes in the wind, but it was only in the *entrée* and *adagio* of the final *pas de deux*, and then in the variation of the Sugar Plum Fairy, that he was able to show himself at somewhere near his best. The *entrée* and *adagio* build up in a marvellous way, with every phrase sensitively attuned to Tchaikovsky's music; and for the Sugar Plum Fairy's variation he devised delicate and charming *pointe*-work and arm movements which caught exactly the filigree charm of Tchaikovsky's music.

The ballet was a deserved failure when first staged in St Petersburg in 1892. However, a great many choreographers have been attracted to the Tchaikovsky music, and have tried to make something stageworthy of the ballet, adapting the story in all sorts of ways. Their success has always been limited, because of the basic defects of the libretto. Sensitive choreographers preserve the

The corps de ballet *swans in* Swan Lake, *Act II. Sadler's Wells Ballet at Covent Garden, c. 1950.*

final *pas de deux*, recognizing that they cannot improve on Ivanov's magical choreography. The ballet, although never intended for children, has now become established as a Christmas entertainment for the young.

A fortunate combination of circumstances enabled Ivanov, before he died, to show his supreme ability by creating Acts II and IV of *Swan Lake*. In this very Russian ballet, he achieved a magical renaissance of romanticism; indeed, *Swan Lake* is the finest of all romantic ballets, in spite of the fact that the acts choreographed by Petipa clash in style with the 'swan' acts, and are of much lower artistic quality. Here was a breakthrough: a ballet of supreme quality, able to challenge comparison with the finest operas and plays, like the best ballets of earlier periods.

Clearly, Ivanov was influenced to some extent by Perrot's choreography for Act II of *Giselle*, with its fluid combination of dances and its romantic dance-images. He was also fortunate in being able to use superb music by Tchaikovsky – written some years earlier, in a free and marvellously expressive way, for a production in Moscow. Tchaikovsky's original score takes no account of the rigid formulas established by Petipa, and shows a close affinity with his operas. In spite of a libretto superbly adapted to ballet as well as the magical music, the ballet had only limited success when first staged in Moscow because of its feeble choreography and inadequate dancing. When Tchaikovsky died, Vsevolozhsky decided that a memorial performance at St Petersburg's Maryinsky Theatre should include a

RIGHT *In Petipa's* Raymonda, *performed by the Bolshoi Ballet in 1963, the Saracen knight Abderahman pays court to Raymonda.*

new version of Act II, the first 'swan' scene. Petipa – presumably daunted by the 'symphonic' nature of the music, which did not remotely resemble anything he had tackled before – assigned this production to Ivanov; and Ivanov – working very rapidly – created the centre of what was to become the most popular of all ballets, as well as the first great Russian ballet.

The development of the choreography of Act II has compelling complexity and fluidity. Ivanov and Tchaikovsky are not telling a story in a way one might expect in a play: what we see is supremely poetic and symbolic, showing the development of the action through dance-images of a new kind. These flower above all in the big *pas de deux*: Odette's arm and head movements

Royal Ballet guest-artist Natalia Makarova dancing Odette in Swan Lake, *Act II. She shows the* dusha *characteristic of the Russian 'school' and essential in* Swan Lake.

project her swan-like nature, suggesting flight on powerful wings, preening feathers, and so on. These dance-images have such nobility that they establish that she is a princess, and such lyrical sadness that they establish the tragic quality of her situation, condemned by the magician to become a swan during the day. Ivanov makes no attempt at naturalistic imitation: when a real swan lands, it does so with a great flurry, whereas the Swan Queen, Odette, comes to rest with a very beautiful kneel on the ground and a bending forward of the trunk and arms. At one point, the *corps de ballet* swans take over the stage, and Odette and Siegfried retreat to the back before launching out on a further development of the *pas de deux*.

Such choreography, with its poetic and highly expressive dance-images and its sensitive musicality, lends itself to many nuances of interpretation: no two great ballerinas perform it in the same way, and some change their interpretation from one performance to the next. The great artist Galina Ulanova, influenced by the fluidity of Ivanov's choreography, developed an interpretation of the big *pas de deux* in which she kept some part of her body in movement throughout; such was the mystery and lyricism she projected that ballerinas all over the world began to dance the *pas de deux* in this way.

The ending of the act is particularly moving, with Odette backing off stage on *pointe* – as she is compelled to leave by the enchantment of the magician – but trailing her arms in mingled hope and despair at the prince who has sworn to release her from the spell.

Judging by the way Act IV emerged when the ballet was revived for the Vic-Wells Ballet in 1934 – providing a model for subsequent productions all over the world – it had much in common with Act II. However, Ninette de Valois, director of the company, disapproved of it, and began to make changes until, eventually, Ivanov's choreography became quite lost. In the Soviet Union, too, there have been countless changes to Act IV – so what we have now is a great variety of new versions of this act. (More recently, the Royal ballet's 1986 production restored as much as possible of the Ivanov choreography.) Fortunately, Ivanov's choreography for Act II is usually retained with only minor changes, and this act is so supreme in its beauty and expressiveness that it carries the rest of the ballet along with it.

Tchaikovsky's music provides for a long scene of mime in Act II in which Odette, using conventional gestures, 'speaks' to Siegfried, explaining to him her sad plight. The gestures signify words: spreading the arms with fluttering hands, for example, signifies a lake. When these gestures are done properly, they carry a charge of feeling, and are perfectly matched to the music. It is common for ballet masters to replace the gestures with dance-images adapted from those devised by Ivanov for other parts of Act II, but this repetition spoils Ivanov's superbly planned structure. Spectators familiar with the ballet relish the mime scene, even if they do not understand all the gestures; they see it as an integral part of the ballet.

CHAPTER SEVEN

Fokine and Diaghilev

Although the great renaissance of ballet in the 20th century is identified outside the Soviet Union with Diaghilev – as the leader of a remarkable group of artists – it was well under way in pre-Revolutionary Russia before Diaghilev presented his first season in Paris.

In its early years, the renaissance had two main aspects, closely associated with each other. One was the rise of the Russian 'school' of ballet, and the appearance of a galaxy of great dancers who were exponents of this 'school'. The other was the emergence of a choreographer of genius, Mikhail Fokine – who took over from Ivanov a few years after the latter died in 1901.

For many years, two 'schools' of ballet technique had been taught in St Petersburg: the old French 'school', distinguished by its elegance and restraint; and the more recently perfected Italian 'school', distinguished by its power and the clarity with which the different limbs were coordinated. The chief teacher of the old French 'school' was Christian Johansson, who had brought the style with him from Stockholm in 1841. The Italian 'school' was introduced by a series of outstanding Italian ballerinas and by the dancer Enrico Cecchetti, who began to teach in St Petersburg in 1892. A rising generation of highly gifted dancers combined aspects of these two 'schools' (some went to Milan to study with Catarina Beretta), and thus made it possible for Fokine to create choreography of a new type, with poetic, highly condensed and wonderfully expressive dance-images: first in the solo he created for Anna Pavlova, *Le Cygne* (*The Dying Swan*, 1907); and then in the second version of *Chopiniana* (*Les Sylphides*, 1909), with Pavlova, Olga Preobrazhenskaya, Vaslav Nijinsky and Tamara Karsavina. With these two intensely original works, Fokine lifted the art of ballet back to the same level as that attained by Tchaikovsky and Ivanov in Act II of *Swan Lake*. In addition, the new Russian 'school' was superbly displayed, in all its breadth and poetry, bringing together the best qualities of the French and Italian 'schools', and projecting a very Russian quality of *dusha*.

Like Bournonville and Perrot, Fokine was in love with his favourite dancer, Pavlova, who was his muse, his inspiration. In *Le Cygne* he gave her the opportunity to interpret, in the most touching way, the struggles against death of a dying swan. Using music by Saint-Saëns, he presented the choreographic equivalent of a swan song, with expression mainly concentrated in the arms, head and trunk. In *Chopiniana*, using an orchestrated version of pieces by Chopin, he gave her a very romantic *pas de deux* with Nijinsky, with lifts of a totally new kind. Other solo pieces in *Chopiniana* were in the same general style, but were different in mood: the waltz was full of gaiety (with quick little steps breaking away from the classroom), the first mazurka had the *danseuse* floating through the air in high leaps, the second mazurka showed the man as a poet, and the prelude was mysterious, as if the *danseuse* were searching for something. ('The echo of a sigh' was how Fokine once described the object of her search.) Throughout the ballet, Fokine used the music with new freedom, respecting the romantic nuances of Chopin and adding some of his own.

In his first ballet for the Maryinsky repertoire, *The Animated Gobelins*, Fokine was clearly aware that ballet in the 20th century needed to be far more concentrated than before. The libretto by Alexandre Benois – a member of a group associated with Diaghilev – was in three acts, but Fokine insisted on cutting it down to one. In the Benois

ABOVE *Magically colourful and exotic design by Léon Bakst for* Schéhérazade. *Diaghilev Ballets Russes, 1910.*

LEFT *Vaslav Nijinsky as the Golden Slave in* Schéhérazade. *Diaghilev Ballets Russes. Painting by George Barbier.*

ABOVE *Design by Alexandre Benois for the fairground scenes in* Petrushka. *The white stagecloth (suggesting snow) helps to give mystery as Diaghilev's lighting suggests the fall of night. Diaghilev Ballets Russes, 1911.*
RIGHT *The costume designed by Léon Bakst for Petrushka, Diaghilev Ballets Russes, 1910. Photograph by Lausat.*

libretto, the Vicomte de Beaugency takes refuge in the castle of a magician. There he sees a Gobelin tapestry depicting Armida and her court. He falls asleep, and in his dream Armida and the other figures come to life.

Now, at last, Fokine was able to realize his dream of collaborating with other creative artists. He worked very closely with Benois on the costumes and complex scene-changes, and also with the composer Tcherepnine. Tamara Karsavina, as Armida, danced with grace and mystery, and Nijinsky (as Armida's slave) rose in marvellously soft vertical leaps.

Diaghilev's role in the extraordinarily rapid development of the art of ballet in the early decades of the century was like that of Count Durazzo: he was a creative artistic director, bringing together groups of outstandingly gifted artists on a series of projects, ensuring a high degree of coordination, and raising the necessary money. Thus ballets became once again complete

Fokine's Le Spectre de la rose, *as performed by the Diaghilev Ballets Russes in 1911, with Nijinsky in the title role and Karsavina as the dreaming young girl.*

works of art, with every detail making its due contribution to the total effect. With him as leader of the teams – and with the finest Russian dancers (on summer holiday) – a series of masterpieces were seen outside Russia which taught the world that ballet, far from being a minor art, could give a lead to all the arts.

For his first Paris season of Russian opera and ballet in 1909, Diaghilev presented little that was new. He took three of Fokine's existing ballets (which he renamed *Le Pavillon d'Armide*, *Les Sylphides* and *Cléopâtre*), commissioned him to create a revised version of the Polovtsian Dances from the opera *Prince Igor*, and had magical new scenery and costumes designed for all his productions. The season was an overwhelming success, and launched Diaghilev and his colleagues on international careers in a new world of ballet that they themselves had created. From now on, they staged ballets which could never have been accepted for performance by the Imperial Russian Ballet at the Maryinsky Theatre.

His realization of Stravinsky's potential as a ballet composer, and his commission for *The Firebird*, was a further demonstration of Diaghilev's astounding creativity. This ballet was remarkable in that Fokine had to come to terms with music of a new kind, by a man would become one of the greatest ballet composers of all time. While parts of this work – notably the dances of the demons – eventually began to look dated, this has never been true of the role of the Firebird: Fokine had Karsavina dance this with great power, in a rather oriental way, and she created a new kind of romantic mystery which still retains all its appeal.

Schéhérazade was by no means so advanced in its choreography, but it did have a superb role for Nijinsky, who projected animal-like passion as the Golden Slave. What is more, this ballet had sets and costumes by the Russian painter Léon Bakst, who used strong, exotic colours to create a scenic atmosphere unlike anything seen before.

In 1911, Diaghilev formed a permanent company – the Ballets Russes – with Nijinsky (probably the greatest male dancer who has ever lived) at its head. When Diaghilev brought together Stravinsky, Benois and Fokine for *Petrushka*, this ballet, with the leading roles performed by Nijinsky, Karsavina, Alexander Orlov and Cecchetti, proved to be one of the greatest ever produced, with perfect harmony between all the elements. It demands a very great artist to interpret the title role, that of a puppet hopelessly in love with another doll, the vain and naive Ballerina, and passionately in revolt against the puppeteer: if Petrushka is danced by such an artist, and the other solo parts are well performed, the ballet never fails to fascinate the audience. Fokine could never have created this central role, breaking free into a new world of choreographic expression, without the collaboration of Nijinsky – able to suggest a sensitive man with an unattractive body, crazed by the fact that his beloved prefers someone stupid but glamorous.

When Diaghilev was asked what his contribution to a ballet had been, he was inclined to reply, 'I did the lighting.' To his questioners, this must have seemed ludicrous false modesty, but there was much truth in Diaghilev's reply. His lighting of *Petrushka* was complex and poetic, creating just the right atmosphere at each moment.

Fokine demonstrated very emphatically the concentrated nature of the new type of ballet by creating a wonderfully romantic work for just two great dancers: *Le Spectre de la rose*, with Nijinsky and Karsavina. This ballet was short, but totally satisfying – with Nijinsky moving in a new way, drooping his hands as he floated through the air so as to suggest the petals and scent of a rose, and Karsavina projecting with delightful simplicity an innocent young girl returning from her first ball, and having a fantastic dream.

CHAPTER EIGHT

Later Diaghilev Choreographers

Not content with stunning spectators with the masterpieces of Fokine, Diaghilev now devoted his immense energy and his expertise in all the arts to fostering the development of Nijinsky as his second choreographer. This was very hard on Fokine: without the great artists of the Ballets Russes he was crippled. But Diaghilev was determined to keep up a vertiginous pace of artistic advance, and gave Nijinsky all the time he needed for his totally novel ballets, so different from anything seen before that they might have come from another planet.

In *L'Après-midi d'un faune*, the great dancer revealed himself as the first expressionist choreographer. The most astonishing thing about this ballet is that Nijinsky, who as a dancer was able to produce an incomparable flow of movement, chose to exclude all fluidity from his new ballet. The movements he wanted for the nymphs, akin to those he created for himself as the faun, were angular and abrupt, with the body kept in profile, and broke clean away from the classroom ballet steps. To achieve the desired results, he needed a great many rehearsals, demonstrating over and over again what he wanted. Fortunately, he had in his cast his sister Bronislava, who was deeply attuned to him and his ideas.

The music selected by Diaghilev – Claude Debussy's *Prélude à l'après-midi d'un faune* – was not in the least expressionistic, being dreamy and impressionistic. The scenery designed by Bakst included an idealized semi-abstract landscape as backcloth. His costume for Nijinsky was astoundingly original: a skintight body suit, covered with dark blotches, a bunch of grapes at the groin, and a headdress suggesting horns. The nymphs wore beautifully draped robes suggesting archaic Greece. Strangely, all these disparate elements fused together in the performance, and the bizarre nature of the mixture gave added mystery to the unusual theme – the half-awakened sexual desires of an adolescent, treated symbolically as those of a young faun in ancient Greece.

Fortunately, the ballet did not fall into oblivion, like the other Nijinsky ballets: it was preserved in the Diaghilev repertoire, and in 1931, Marie Rambert had Leon Woizikowski (who had joined the Ballets Russes in 1915) stage it for her

Nijinsky's L'Après-midi d'un faune, *with Nijinsky dancing the title role for the Diaghilev Ballets Russes in 1912. Lydia Nelidova is the chief nymph. Drawing after Valentine Gross.*

LEFT *Rudolf Nureyev in the title role in the Nijinsky ballet* L'Après-midi d'un faune, *with Alexandra Wells as the leading nymph. Ballet-Théâtre Français de Nancy, Edinburgh Festival, 1987.*
CENTRE *The Adolescent Girls in Nijinsky's* The Rite of Spring, *as performed in Paris in 1913. The inturned feet and stylized make-up are characteristic features of this epoch-making ballet.*

company. This production was filmed, which made it possible to revive it many years later. Its magical quality emerges clearly when a sensitive dancer takes the role of the faun.

Nijinsky's expressionism could be seen even more clearly in *Le Sacre du printemps* (*The Rite of Spring*, 1913), with another Stravinsky score of the utmost rhythmic complexity. This needed hundreds of rehearsals, for it was far more difficult than *L'Après-midi d'un faune*, and Nijinsky had to demonstrate what he wanted to a large number of dancers. The ballet was given only seven performances, for Diaghilev rejected Nijinsky after he got married, but hundreds of drawings make it clear that it represented a major leap forward in the art.

Avoiding the *plié* used with small jumps up to then, Nijinsky suggested primitive rituals by having the dancers land with stiff knees; their bodies were also twisted in amazing ways. He was much helped by Marie Rambert, whom Diaghilev had brought from the school of Eurythmics in Germany directed by Emile Jaques-Dalcroze. She went over with him every night the music he planned to use the following day, and figured out the counts he would give to the dancers, so that they could find their way amid Stravinsky's extremely complicated rhythms. Nijinsky worked every aspect of the music into his choreography – for example, staging contrapuntal patterns of group movement (and of the parts of the bodies of the dancers) which corresponded to contrapuntal patterns in the music. In working out these patterns, he was helped by Marie Rambert, for Dalcroze had his students interpret counterpoint in just this way.

Nijinsky staged a number of ritualistic group dances in the earlier sections of the ballet, including line, chain and circular dances – using patterns to be found in folk dances around the world. The steps were not derived from folk dances, however: the dancers stamped and shuffled in an angular, grotesque way and, of course, avoided the *plié* when they landed from jumps. After the Chosen Maiden was selected by the elders of the tribe, she stood still while the other dancers moved around her. For her solo, she used stiffly angled arms which harked back to the position of Petrushka's

in his cell: Nijinsky had poured a great deal of his own feelings into that role, influencing Fokine's development of the choreography, and it was natural for him to look back to it when choreographing the role of the Chosen Maiden. (Being unable, as a man, to dance this role himself, he created it for his sister Bronislava, much like him in temperament and physique; to his annoyance, he found that her pregnancy prevented her from dancing it at the première.)

The dancers' make-up was highly stylized, in an expressionist way; and the designer Nicholas Roerich – an expert in folklore and archaeology – evoked ancient Russia with his costumes, pointed hats and taped shoes suggesting those worn by Russian peasants. He used only stark colours in the scenery – with bright greens at first, suggesting the coming of spring, and darker hues for the scene of ritual sacrifice.

Much to Diaghilev's delight, the first performance of the ballet in Paris caused a riot: the noise from the audience was so great that it drowned the music, and Nijinsky had to shout the counts to the dancers from the wings. This was probably the most extraordinary evening in the history of ballet: the combination of Stravinsky's score – which still sounds astonishingly challenging today – and Nijinsky's equally original choreography gave the spectators a shattering experience.

By now, Diaghilev had achieved such wonders that he believed he could create choreographers just as he wished, and he decided to make an inexperienced young dancer, Léonide Massine (who had a limited technique but great charisma), the successor to Nijinsky, who had infuriated Diaghilev by getting married.

The break with Diaghilev had a shattering effect on Nijinsky's career as a choreographer. Without the marvellous Diaghilev dancers, he found it difficult to create further ballets, and then he was interned in Hungary as an alien. By the time he created *Tyl Eulenspiegel* with the Diaghilev Ballets Russes in 1916, he was already going mad, and he gave his last performance for Diaghilev the following year.

Diaghilev's confidence in his own flair for talent proved to be justified: Massine achieved enormous fame, creating a series of ballets for the Diaghilev Ballets Russes in the latter part of the First World War and in the immediate post-war years, and then for the two Ballets Russes de Monte Carlo companies which did their best to carry on the Diaghilev traditon after the impresario's death. Massine's ballets were greatly successful for many years – indeed, he came to be widely accepted as the supreme choreographer of his day – but after some decades, when they were produced by other companies, most of them had lost their appeal. Without the supreme artists who had created the leading roles – Lydia Lopokova, Massine himself, Alexandra Danilova, Irina Baronova, Yurek Shabelevsky and several others – they showed a certain mechanical quality: it was as if they had been created by a skilfully programmed computer.

The trouble was that Massine was, at heart, an expressionist, but rarely created expressionist choreography. When he did – as in the new version of *Le Sacre du printemps* that he created for Diaghilev in 1920, drawing to some extent on the

memories of dancers who had performed in the original Nijinsky production – Massine was even more expressionist than his predecessor had been. In the scene of sacrifice, for example, he had the Chosen Maiden stand still for fifteen minutes in a very contorted position before beginning her solo – one which made great demands on her stamina. Fortunately, Lydia Sokolova (a great English dancer who had become completely Russianized) gloried in the extreme demands which Massine made on her – flinging herself to the ground, and whirling around the stage in a *manège* of *coupés-jetés* during which she had to keep her head tilted to one side, with her arms contorted, and her hands folded into fists. Massine's treatment of the music for this solo was expressionistic, though not in the usual way (hitting each beat with demonic accuracy). In fact, he had Sokolova ignore the music completely, right up to the end – when she had two chords in which to adjust her timing to that of the music, before her final collapse into death. (Here Massine tried too hard to be avant-garde: when Sokolova later taught the dance to Anne Heaton for a British television programme, she adjusted the timing of the steps so that they fitted Stravinsky's powerful rhythms – and then the dance looked even better.)

Despite its expressionism, the Massine version of *The Rite of Spring* did not appear shocking after the horrors of the First World War, and it was so popular with audiences that it stayed in the repertoire right up to the dissolution of the

LEFT *The talented ballerina Fiona Chadwick as the Chosen Maiden in Kenneth MacMillan's version of* The Rite of Spring, *with striking decor and costumes by the Australian artist Sidney Nolan. Royal Ballet, 1987 revival.*

RIGHT *Léonide Massine as the cobbler in the film* The Red Shoes *(1948), presenting the dancing shoes he has made. Massine created the choreography for his own role.*

BELOW RIGHT *Final scene of* Les Noces, *with choreography by Bronislava Nijinska for Diaghilev, 1923. Re-staged by her for Royal Ballet, 1966. With her ballet preserved, she said: 'Now I can die happy.'*

Diaghilev company. Another splendid foray into expressionism was made by Massine in 1919 when he created for himself the *farruca* in *The Three-Cornered Hat* (*Le Tricorne*). This was based on the authentic traditional Spanish dance in Flamenco style – itself very expressionistic – and Massine skilfully adapted it to suit his own incomplete but powerful ballet technique, dancing with the right *duende*.

This ballet rejoiced in one of the most poetic of all ballet settings – designed by Picasso with the bold simplicity of genius, and using wide areas of flat colour in a way quite new to scenic design. With this marvellously original scenery, the intensely Spanish music by Manuel de Falla, an admirable libretto based on a play by Gregorio Martínez Sierra, and the splendidly balletized *farruca*, this ballet deserves preservation.

Bronislava Nijinska (Vaslav's sister) was fortunate (and so are we) in that her two best ballets have survived. *Les Noces* (*The Wedding*), staged in 1923 after a long delay, had a magnificent score by Stravinsky that was related to his equally remarkable music for *The Rite of Spring*. The ballet belonged in style and spirit to the pre-war golden age of the company; in it, Nijinska showed that she had a profound understanding of her brother's work on *The Rite of Spring*. *Les Noces*, concerned with ancient wedding customs, had an austere, ritualistic quality, and its rhythms were superbly matched to those of the music. The sets and costumes designed by Natalia Goncharova

Svetlana Beriosova showing witty sophistication as the Hostess in Bronislava Nijinska's Les Biches. *Royal Ballet at Covent Garden, c. 1964.*

were also admirably in harmony with the archaic quality of the Stravinsky score.

Les Biches (1924) could hardly have been more different in style and theme. It matched exactly the cosmopolitan, sophisticated atmosphere of the Ballets Russes during this period, when contact with Russia had been lost and Diaghilev was desperately attempting to keep up with the latest Parisian ideas instead of giving a lead, as happened before the war. The ballet was both frivolous and satirical in a highly sophisticated way; it showed three athletes totally involved with each other (and their muscles), a pair of adolescent lesbian lovers, a sexually ambiguous woman dressed as a page boy, and a fashionable hostess with a long cigarette holder and a long string of pearls. It was staged with wit and assurance by Nijinska and has never lost its appeal.

George Balanchine, who had left the Soviet Union in 1924 at the head of a small group (including the delightful artist Alexandra Danilova), joined the Diaghilev company with his dancers, and was soon appointed chief choreographer. Being young, adaptable, intelligent and versatile, he was able to give Diaghilev exactly what he wanted in the last years of his life. Balanchine's ballets for Diaghilev were bizarre for the time, avoiding normal expectations and often showing a deliberate disharmony between their constituent elements. They might have been invented in response to a famous remark made by Diaghilev to Jean Cocteau at an earlier date: '*Etonne-moi!*' ('Astonish me!').

The most successful of Balanchine's ballets for Diaghilev was *The Prodigal Son*, in which the ancient story was treated in a highly sophisticated manner; it was so skilfully provocative that it has never lost its popularity. Diaghilev was delighted with it, especially since its title role, a long and exhausting one, was created for the beautiful and charismatic young dancer Serge Lifar, with whom he was in love.

Diaghilev, a diabetic, refused to keep to the strict diet necessary for those suffering from this disease, and died in Venice in 1929. Without him the company came to an end.

CHAPTER NINE

Pavlova

Anna Pavlova's contribution to the popularization of ballet was unique. She was driven by an obsession: to dance all over the world, in as many cities and towns as possible, to perform for as many people as possible. No town was too small or remote, no theatre too unsuited, and as a result, she introduced ballet to millions. Even when the small town of Guayaquil in Ecuador was stricken with yellow fever, she insisted on performing there – ignoring the danger to herself and her dancers. She herself summed up her obsession: 'I want to dance to everyone in the world.'

In one week, at the start of a British tour, she performed in seven towns and cities on the south coast, giving two performances in different places in one day. But this was only the beginning. During the next nine weeks, she performed in a total of forty-two cities in England, Scotland and Wales. During her incessant travels, she performed in every possible type of venue – from the grandest opera houses to grubby halls. Her stamina was incredible: she worked her dancers hard, but she worked much harder herself, determined to maintain her standard of performance at the highest possible level. Being human, she did have her 'off' nights, but after the curtain fell, she would make up for any performance that was below par by building up her bows with such skill that she could convince spectators that they had seen something wonderful.

Pavlova in Autumn Leaves *(1919), the only ballet choreographed by her. As a chrysanthemum, she is buffeted to death by the wind, although a poet (Aubrey Hitchins) tries to help her.*

LEFT *Anna Pavlova as the Dying Swan. The photo shows her becoming a legend in her lifetime – with her tutu arranged as a kind of halo, and a circle of laurel leaves around the photo.*
OPPOSITE BELOW *The very moving ending of* The Dying Swan. *Pavlova's hands and extended foot cease to tremble, and the spotlight goes out. Regrettably, the filmed 'takes' stopped before this crucial moment.*

Being such a supreme artist – one of the founders of the Russian 'school', a prima ballerina who could project her dancing superbly to everyone in an audience – she had no need to fear the competition of her rivals. Yet she chose to make her headquarters at Ivy House in London, and to employ English dancers, whom she knew could be induced to dance in a disciplined but routine way, offering her no competition. (In fact, some did have real talent, but this only flowered after they left her company.) Pavlova made an exception with the male dancers who partnered her: they had to be talented dancers to do so effectively and show her to good advantage.

Her determination to surpass all possible rivals became apparent very early in her career. After the young Tamara Karsavina, beginning to take solo roles, had danced a *pas de deux* with Nijinsky, Pavlova rushed up to her in a fury and abused her for dancing 'quite naked'. Karsavina was dumbfounded: all that had happened was that a strap had slipped off one shoulder, something of no significance since, at this time, the bodices of costumes were boned. Preobrazhenskaya came to her rescue, telling her to 'sneeze on the viper'. Later, Pavlova perfected her persona: it was as if she was always giving a performance, projecting her chosen image of the gracious prima ballerina at all times. In fact, she did have a generous nature, taking great care of her own dancers and giving help and encouragement to young hopefuls – including future choreographers.

Artistically, her career was a bundle of contradictions. She inspired Fokine to make his breakthrough by creating *Le Cygne* (*The Dying Swan*) and the *pas de deux* in *Chopiniana* (*Les Sylphides*), and she defied the authorities by jumping in to star in his ballet, *Le Pavillon d'Armide*, at the last moment – after Mathilde Kshessinskaya (ex-mistress of the Tsar, and therefore all-powerful) suddenly abandoned the role. Diaghilev naturally invited Pavlova to dance in his epoch-making first season in Paris in 1909, and thought of her as his standard-bearer: the beautiful poster for this season, designed by Serov, showed her in *Les Sylphides*. When the season opened, however, she was on tour with her own company, and she arrived in Paris two weeks after the opening. Inevitably, she triumphed in the *pas de deux* of *Les Sylphides*, as well as in the roles of Ta-Hor in *Cléopâtre* and Armida in *Le Pavillon d'Armide*, which she had created for Fokine.

From then on, however, Pavlova considered herself and Diaghilev as rivals. She went her own way, often performing conventional, sentimental roles that were unworthy of her but which she transformed by her inspired dancing. She was well aware that *The Dying Swan*, the superbly inventive piece created by Fokine with her help, was a masterpiece of original choreography, but she was content to leave it in solitary glory, to be performed as the climax to her programmes.

Even so, she did continue as an artistic pioneer in some ways. Her own performance in *Giselle* was magical, and she boldly changed the atmosphere of Act II by having the Wilis dressed in shrouds – thus making herself stand out among them. In her appreciation of oriental dance, she showed the same prescience as Fokine and Nijinsky; unlike them, however, she tried very hard to come to terms with authentic oriental dances. In Japan, she commissioned Kabuki masters to stage for her dancers authentic Kabuki pieces. She failed in her attempt to track down authentic classical Indian dances, but showed extraordinary insight in choosing the Indian art student, Uday Shankar, to create two Indian ballets for her company in London, with herself and Shankar dancing the leading roles in one of them (*Krishna and Radha*). While touring with Pavlova, Shankar learned how to administer a dance company; after leaving her, he perfected his own eclectic style of Indian dance and followed Pavlova's example, introducing Indian dance to great numbers of people in many countries.

Pavlova's untimely death at the age of 50 in 1931 came about because of the same obsession which had driven her throughout her life. She insisted on travelling to The Hague for the start of a fresh tour with her company, even though she had been weakened by a short illness, as well as by the enormous strain she had put on her body for so many years. It would have been easy for her to cancel the opening performances and delay her departure, but that was not her way.

We cannot achieve a clear idea of the quality of the dancing of great artists like Nijinsky and Karsavina, but a film of Pavlova in *The Dying Swan* preserves enough of her magic for us to understand why she became a legend in her lifetime, and why her legend has continued to grow since her death.

CHAPTER TEN

The Renaissance of British Ballet

After the death of Diaghilev, his company dissolved, and it looked as if the art of ballet had suffered a death-blow. However, in the vacuum left by Diaghilev's Ballets Russes, two remarkable women – Marie Rambert and Ninette de Valois – achieved between them a renaissance in British ballet.

Foreign choreographers such as Noverre, Didelot and Perrot had done fine things in London, and English and Irish dancers such as Lydia Sokolova, Anton Dolin and Alicia Markova (adopting Russian-sounding names) had taken leading roles in Diaghilev ballets. Despite this, there had been no major developments in British ballet since the pioneering of John Weaver, early in the 18th century. However, once it had been re-established, British ballet forged ahead at a great rate, and led the world in creativity for many years. The fact that these dancers (who also included Marie Rambert and Ninette de Valois) had worked for Diaghilev was of great importance: they knew what it was like to contribute to the work of a great company.

Marie Rambert, who was born in Poland, but moved to England at the outbreak of the First World War, had worked with Nijinsky on *Le Sacre du printemps* – one of the most challenging of all the Diaghilev ballets – drawing on her superb musicality; and she soon proved herself as a creative artistic director of her company (the

LEFT *Soloists posed in Antony Tudor's* Jardin aux lilas *(Ballet Rambert, 1936): Caroline (Maude Lloyd) is torn between her lover (Hugh Laing) and her fiancé (Tudor), who rejects his mistress (Peggy van Praagh).*
RIGHT *In* Checkmate *the Irish-born choreographer Ninette de Valois has the Black Queen lifted by two black knights. Revival by Sadler's Wells Ballet at Covent Garden, 1947.*

Ballet Club). She would allow no ballet on the stage – that of the Mercury Theatre, where her husband Ashley Dukes presented plays – unless it had freshness, individuality and professional polish. As a result, she was able to produce a constantly growing repertoire of fine British ballets – and very few failures. This was an extraordinary achievement. The atmosphere she created was so stimulating that such dancers as Karsavina and Lopokova, who had been stars of Diaghilev's Ballets Russes, were happy to dance for Rambert and stage for her 19th-century classics and Fokine ballets. It was quite characteristic of Rambert that in 1931, soon after forming her company on a permanent basis, she had the fine Diaghilev dancer Woizikowski produce *L'Après-midi d'un*

The atmosphere and style of Tudor's austere masterpiece Dark Elegies *is evoked by this specially posed photo. (L to r) Tudor, Lloyd, van Praagh, de Mille, Walter Gore. Ballet Rambert, 1937.* BELOW RIGHT *The Rose Adagio of Petipa's* The Sleeping Beauty, *with which the Sadler's Wells Ballet triumphantly took over Covent Garden in 1946. Margot Fonteyn as Princess Aurora.*

faune for her.

Her first choreographer was Frederick Ashton, who had been trained by her; she encouraged him to try his hand at choreography as early as 1926. Ashton was deeply influenced by Bronislava Nijinska, and carried on the tradition of the later Diaghilev years of witty, light-hearted ballets. His talent soon flowered in *Façade* (1931), inspired by a witty suite composed by William Walton that was derived from the music he had written to accompany poems by Edith Sitwell. Diaghilev had planned to use Ashton as a choreographer – and he would certainly have appreciated the charm of *Façade*, with its gentle satire of various types of social dances, as well as its musicality. *Façade* was created for a performance at a West End theatre sponsored by the Camargo Society, which was formed with the dual purposes of filling the gap left at Diaghilev's death and encouraging British dancers and choreographers. Ashton used Rambert dancers, with Lopokova as guest artist; *Façade* then entered the repertoires of both the Ballet Club and the Vic-Wells Ballet.

Life was hard for Rambert's choreographers and dancers, for both the auditorium and stage of the Mercury Theatre were tiny, and there was no money to pay the dancers: box-office receipts, takings at the bar and subscriptions to the club were ploughed back into new ballets. The company was called the Ballet Club (except when on tour, when it was the Ballet Rambert) for it usually performed on Sundays, and those buying tickets had to be club members. Because of the lack of finance, many Rambert dancers were lured away to the Vic-Wells Ballet (directed by Ninette de Valois), which paid wages; indeed, the majority of the latter's leading soloists came from the Ballet Club. In 1935, Ashton too joined the Vic-Wells Ballet, becoming its chief choreographer.

His departure did not cripple the Ballet Club, for a choreographer of genius was rapidly maturing at the Mercury Theatre: Antony Tudor. Showing astonishing independence, he broke clean away from the frivolous late-Diaghilev style and produced ballets in which the themes were treated seriously, whether they were comic, tragic or concerned with moods and temperament. The influences on him were manifold – the writer Proust, authentic Kabuki dancing, eclectic Indian dance, modern dance and much else – and his musicality was so wide ranging and so profound that he was able to do quite new things with the relationship of music and dance, creating dance-images of the greatest originality and expressiveness. His first masterpiece was very French and very Proustian: *Jardin aux lilas* (*Lilac Garden*, 1936). This evoked the fast-changing moods of people at a moonlit, lilac-scented garden party; the most subtle and fleeting episodes created a powerful atmosphere, while the tragedy of Caroline – forced to say goodbye to her lover and marry a man she does not love – was contrasted with the bitterness of the rejected mistress of her fiancé. Although the ballet had a running time of under

20 minutes, its choreography was so concentrated, and so intricately matched to the impressionistic music by Ernest Chausson, that it seemed to last much longer – and Tudor altered the flow at one point to show Caroline (danced by Maude Lloyd) taking farewell of her world while all the others at the party were frozen in time. The dancers who matured in this and other Tudor ballets, and were rehearsed by him, became magnificent artists. They learned to sing the music to themselves, carefully avoiding counting its beats – something fatal in a Tudor ballet.

His second masterpiece could hardly have been more different in style and theme. This was *Dark Elegies* (1937), with its austere treatment of a tragic theme: in a poor northern fishing village, all the children have been drowned, and are mourned by their grief-stricken parents. The dance-images were quite unlike any seen before, and were even more concentrated and expressive than those in *Jardin aux lilas*.

Characteristically, Tudor used *Kindertotenlieder* (*Songs on the Death of Children*), a song-cycle by Gustav Mahler – a composer then almost unknown outside Austria and Germany – and showed complete command of this complex music. In the First Song, for example, he had the soloist (Peggy van Praagh) portray a stoic: inward-turned movements showed her crushed by the terrible blow of fate, while outward movements suggested that she would come through.

Outgrowing the Ballet Club, Tudor established his own company, the London Ballet, at the theatre of Toynbee Hall in the East End. He now began to build a varied repertoire with some extraordinary ballets – notably *Gala Performance*, in which he satirized in a subtle but acutely observed way three 'schools' of ballet (French, Italian and Russian) and *Judgement of Paris*, in which he transformed the ancient Greek myth into a sordid episode in a brothel, with the *filles de joie* – looking bored and miserable – making feeble attempts at dancing. The music – from the Brecht–Weill *Threepenny Opera* – was marvellously apt; later, it became very familiar, but at the time it was almost unknown outside Germany. The company was just beginning to establish itself when Tudor accepted an offer to take part in the foundation of Ballet Theatre in New York, thinking that he could return after six months. However, the outbreak of war disrupted his plans, and instead, he played a role of the greatest importance in the rise of American ballet.

The Vic-Wells Ballet – the company founded by Ninette de Valois that performed first at both the Old Vic and Sadler's Wells theatres, and then only at Sadler's Wells – developed in a rather different way; for example, the soloists came mainly from outside, notably from the Ballet Club. De Valois took advantage of the funds at her disposal and the size of the theatre (1,500 seats, compared with 144 at the Mercury) to commission Nicholas Serguéeff (previously *régisseur* and then director of the Imperial Russian Ballet in St Petersburg) to revive most of the classics surviving from the 19th century: *Swan Lake*, *Coppélia*, *The Nutcracker*,

The final scene in a madhouse of Ninette de Valois's ballet The Rake's Progress, *from Hogarth's famous paintings (Vic-Wells Ballet, 1935). The Rake (Robert Helpmann) is put among other madmen.*

Giselle and *The Sleeping Beauty*. With these ballets at the centre of its repertoire, and new ballets by De Valois and Ashton, the company was able to give varied opportunities to its soloists, and they gained steadily in stature. The atmosphere was less stimulating than at the Ballet Club, but some remarkable achievements were made.

One of the most exciting things about the Vic-Wells Ballet in its formative years was the emergence of Margot Fonteyn as a ballerina. It was a major event when she first danced the title role of *Giselle* in 1937: her technique was still faulty, and she could not yet cope with the mystery required in Act II, but in Act I she was marvellous, giving clear promise of future greatness. She was partnered by a very gifted artist from Australia, Robert Helpmann: this admirable partnership lasted for two decades, with Helpmann showing himself as splendidly versatile.

Like Massine and Kurt Jooss, a German modern-dance choreographer – both of whom she greatly admired and by whom she was greatly influenced – De Valois was an expressionist, and when she tackled expressionist themes she did well, notably in *The Rake's Progress* (1935). This was based on a series of paintings by William Hogarth, showing the degeneration of the hero, superbly danced and acted in the ballet by Helpmann. Another fine ballet by her was *Checkmate* (1937), with a skilful transmutation of chess figures into human figures, and a brutal, ferocious ending.

Choreographing for the Vic-Wells Ballet, Ashton showed himself at his witty, light-hearted best in charming ballets such as *Les Rendezvous* (1933) and *Les Patineurs* (*The Skaters*, 1937). He also created romantic ballets for Fonteyn and Helpmann which showed his superb professionalism, even though they did not remain in the repertoire for long.

Dancing every night during the war, instead of just giving two performances each week, the company matured considerably, so that after the war it was able to move to the Royal Opera House, Covent Garden and make it a great home of ballet. (By rights, it should now have been called the Royal Opera and Ballet House.) Now the company – known as the Sadler's Wells Ballet since the beginning of the war – was ready to dance *The Sleeping Beauty* with the right amplitude and spectacle, and with Margot Fonteyn establishing herself unmistakably as a prima ballerina.

Nevertheless, Fonteyn's range was still limited. When Ninette de Valois brought in Serge Grigoriev (who had been Diaghilev's *régisseur-général*) to stage *The Firebird* in 1954, she sensibly asked Karsavina to teach Fonteyn the title role and coach her in it: since Fokine had created the role for Karsavina, she understood it better than anyone. It took a fortnight of rehearsals before Fonteyn began to understand the Fokine choreography and the strange creature she was expected to project, but at the première she gave one of her finest performances. The result was that Fokine's ballet was a triumphant success.

Returning from his service with the RAF during the war, Ashton created a ballet which proved to be a masterpiece: the abstract *Symphonic Variations*, with only six solo dancers, who

Frederick Ashton's abstract ballet Symphonic Variations, *with Karen Paisey, Mark Silver, Wendy Ellis and Cynthia Harvey dancing before the mathematical curves of Sophie Fedorovich's backcloth. Revival by Royal Ballet, 1980.*

are on stage throughout the ballet. Fonteyn was admirable in this cleanly etched and elegant production, bringing together in a fresh way all the *enchaînements* Ashton had perfected in his romantic ballets.

His achievements between 1963 and 1970 were extraordinary. Taking over from De Valois as director of the company (now known as the Royal Ballet), he brought it into a golden age. A number of outstanding ballerinas emerged, he arranged for Bronislava Nijinska to stage her two finest ballets, *Les Biches* and *Les Noces*, and he persuaded Tudor to return to London and create a new masterpiece, the Buddhist ballet *Shadowplay* – which induced the dancers to tackle (with success) dance-images very different from anything they had encountered before. The young Anthony Dowell flowered into a great artist in the central role (in which he suggested a young Buddha), and Merle Park was devastatingly sensual and destructive as a powerful goddess. Tudor also revived *Jardin aux lilas*, with great success, and created a witty and cynical new ballet for the touring company: *Knight Errant*, with David Wall superb as the devil-may-care hero, seducing women for the fun of it.

LEFT *Fokine's* The Firebird, *with Cynthia Harvey in the title role and Anthony Dowell as Ivan Tsarevich. Royal Ballet at Covent Garden, 1987.*
RIGHT *Antoinette Sibley and guest-artist Fernando Bujones in* Jazz Calendar, *with choreography by Kenneth Macmillan. Royal Ballet at Covent Garden, 1985.*

Ashton ceased to be artistic director in 1970, and this in turn brought about the end of the Royal Ballet's Ashtonian golden age. However, he still worked with the company, ensuring that the quality of his own ballets was retained, and in 1976 he showed that he had lost none of his flair for narrative ballets, which he had displayed so admirably in *La Fille mal gardée*. His new ballet, *A Month in the Country*, based on Ivan Turgenev's masterly play of the same name, used the finest artists in the company with skill and imagination to establish the various characters with superb clarity. As a result, the tensions of the play, as well as its comedy, came over vividly. Lynn Seymour brought out exquisitely the maddening contradictions in the character and behaviour of the heroine, Natalia Petrovna; Anthony Dowell was delightfully innocent as the young tutor Beliaev; and Derek Rencher (now concentrating on mime) built up with fine intelligence and restraint the character of Rakitin – a man obsessed with Natalia Petrovna. (In the play, Turgenev was really portraying himself in this role, hopelessly obsessed as he was with Pauline Viardot.)

In May 1988 Ashton's ballet *Ondine* was revived, one of his great three act ballets which could have been lost, since Ashton died later that summer.

The most influential choreographer to emerge within the company after the war was Kenneth Macmillan, who has a flair for creating ingenious solos and *pas de deux*. In *Romeo and Juliet* (1965) – his new version of a ballet planned in detail in Leningrad by the Soviet choreographer Leonid Lavrovsky, who used Prokofiev's score – MacMillan showed his talent at its best. The last act, with Juliet almost constantly on stage, was particularly fine: four ballerinas (Margot Fonteyn, Lynn Seymour, Antoinette Sibley and Merle Park) danced this role at the opening series of performances, and all interpreted it differently.

The company gained much from the inclusion of great artists from abroad. Two superb exponents of the Russian 'school,' Violette Elvin and Svetlana Beriosova, danced with wonderful breadth and lyricism. From Canada came Lynn Seymour, a great dramatic dancer, and Jennifer Penney, delightful in off-beat roles; the great Russian dancer Galina Samsova came to the company after starring elsewhere. From South

LEFT *Jennifer Penney, partnered by Wayne Eagling, shows her elegant legs and flair for zany humour in* La fin du jour, *with choreography by Kenneth MacMillan. Royal Ballet at Covent Garden, 1979.*
RIGHT *Kenneth MacMillan's* Mayerling, *with David Wall as Prince Rudolf and Wendy Ellis as the unfortunate Princess Stephanie, whom he is forced to marry. Royal Ballet at Covent Garden, 1978.*

Africa arrived the *demi-caractère* ballerina Nadia Nerina and the dramatic dancer Monica Mason; from Zimbabwe (then called Rhodesia) came the musical Merle Park, while Alexander Grant, splendid in comic roles, came from New Zealand. And Rudolf Nureyev was enormously influential during the years when he appeared as guest artist with Margot Fonteyn, inspiring her to dance with new freshness and himself displaying the glories of the Russian 'school'. His dancing stimulated the male dancers of the company, and did much to put male dancing back in the forefront.

One of the finest male dancers to emerge within the Royal Ballet – at any time since its formation in 1931 – was David Wall. Here was an artist of extraordinary grace, intelligence and stage presence, one who gave individuality to every role he tackled. With his elegant body and handsome features, he was ideal in romantic roles – but he was no less superb in comic and dramatic ones. Although Tudor had shown as early as 1971 that Wall could work in a creative way on new roles, the company choreographers tended to pass him over; but in 1978 Kenneth MacMillan gave him the leading role of Prince Rudolf in his new ballet *Mayerling*. Wall interpreted this long, complex and very challenging role with such intensity – showing the gradual degeneration of the Prince into a man so desperate that he killed himself – that the ballet made a striking impact. As Prince Rudolf, Wall was unforgettable and irreplaceable.

Anthony Dowell took over as artistic director of the Company in 1986. Dancers of his quality are very rare, and although he felt he had to cut down the number of his performances, the fact that he continued to dance did much for the Company.

David Bintley stood out in the boldest way among the young dancers of the company who began to create ballets in the late 1970s and 1980s. Bintley's talent as a choreographer was obvious, but for some years he seemed to find difficulty in achieving a voice of his own in the many ballets he created for the Sadler's Wells Royal Ballet and the Royal Ballet. It was in his dancing of the role of Petrushka that he showed his creative powers at full stretch, reshaping the ballet as a masterpiece. Bintley was appointed Resident Choreographer of the Royal Ballet in 1986.

In 1988 he showed an individual and delightful sense of humour in his new ballet *'Still Life' at the Penguin Café*, which was a series of quirky sketches involving animals and birds. These ended with the splendid artist Stephen Jefferies making a good deal of the role of a monkey. Gifted with a keen sense of style, and being wonderfully versatile, Jefferies has always shown himself able to cope admirably with a wide variety of roles.

The Ballet Rambert did well for some years after the war, even though its subsidy from the British government (via the Arts Council) was too small. In 1960, Marie Rambert commissioned an admirable production of Bournonville's *La Sylphide* from Elsa-Marianne von Rosen who, drawing on extensive research, by herself and her husband Alan Fridericia, was able to fill in some gaps. The Australian dancer Lucette Aldous was polished and delightful in the title role, though her style was not quite authentically Bournonvillean. At the annual seasons at Sadler's Wells, Rambert took pride in presenting all-Tudor programmes with Gillian Martlew and Anna Truscott doing wonders with challenging roles. Rambert's success in maintaining high standards in *Gala Performance* and *Judgement of Paris* was extraordinary, even if nuances were lost in *Jardin aux lilas* and *Dark Elegies*.

Costs, however, kept rising, and it became impossible to maintain a ballet company large enough to perform the classics. The associate director, Norman Morrice, therefore transformed the company in 1966 into a modern-dance company – abandoning the old repertoire and giving Glen Tetley and others the opportunity to stage a new kind of ballet.

The London Festival Ballet was established by Anton Dolin and Alicia Markova in 1949, with a *corps de ballet* comprising students from the Arts Educational School. The programmes they gave were so successful that Dolin was encouraged to found a permanent company, with himself as artistic director and Julian Braunsweg as manager – coping with all the problems involved in running a ballet company as a commercial venture, without subsidy (which was still possible at this time). A new Markova was revealed – dancing with elegance and purity of line – for a few years. The company toured widely, like the Ballets Russes de Monte Carlo companies, and was very like them in character, performing much the same repertoire, and bringing in a great many guest artists. Massine's 1950 production of *Petrushka* – with the choreographer himself in the title role, and the great French artist Yvette Chauviré as the Ballerina – was masterly.

Markova left the company in 1952, and Dolin in 1961, when Braunsweg took over completely as both director and business manager. There was a

long series of artistic directors, and as a consequence, the artistic standard went up and down, and so did the finances. No new ballets of any importance were created for the company, although Jack Carter's highly professional and strongly dramatic ballet *The Witch Boy* (originally created for a Dutch ballet company) provided a valuable addition to the repertoire, as did the Danish choreographer Harald Lander's *Etudes*, devised as a showpiece for the Royal Danish Ballet.

Between 1968 and 1979, the artistic standard improved so much under the artistic direction of Beryl Grey that the LFB rivalled the Royal Ballet, which was no longer directed by Ashton. Her two most remarkable achievements were to bring in the great young ballerina Eva Evdokimova as a regular guest artist – in effect, a member of the company – and to commission from the Danish dancer Peter Schaufuss a splendid production of *La Sylphide*. His version, which incorporated much research by his parents (both experts in Bournonville traditions) as well as his own ideas, is masterly in concept and execution, with gaps in the traditional choreography filled in with surviving fragments by Bournonville.

Eva Evdokimova – who had been trained in the Bournonville 'school' in Copenhagen after being trained in London – gave the title role such charm, pathos, humour, musicality, lightness and perfection of line that she made it easy to understand why Grahn and the other superstars who had

LEFT *Stephen Jefferies as the Monkey in* 'Still Life' at the Penguin Café, *with choreography by David Bintley. Première by Royal Ballet at Covent Garden, 1988.*

TOP *Bournonville's* La Sylphide, *staged for Ballet Rambert by Elsa Marianne von Rosen. Shown on BBC TV, 1961, with Australian Lucette Aldous in the title role and Danish Flemming Flindt as James.*

ABOVE *Jack Carter's* Witch Boy, *performed by London Festival Ballet in 1958. John Gilpin – as splendid as the Witch Boy as in classical roles – is given life by the Conjur Man.*

LEFT *The climax of the Schaufuss production of* La Sylphide *for London Festival Ballet. Eva Evdokimova (as the dying sylph) is deeply moving, while James (Peter Schaufuss) kneels in despair.*

appeared in the original version of this romantic ballet had been idolized by the public. Schaufuss danced James with the right authority, brilliance and authenticity of style; and the Danish guest artist Niels Bjørn Larsen, as the vicious witch Madge, gave a memorable demonstration of the powerful Bournonville mime tradition, involving hardly any use of conventional gestures.

Derek Bailey, a BBC director with a flair for working in ballet, translated this production of *La Sylphide* splendidly on to television screens. He prepared his shooting script with the greatest care, making up a storyboard with the help of the company's Benesh-trained dance notator, and taped the ballet as it was performed in the London Coliseum before an invited audience. In this way, he managed to get exactly what he wanted in each shot, and the dancers were able to dance and act with all the spontaneity of a 'live' performance. Indeed, tears could be seen in Evdokimova's eyes in her very moving death scene, with the camera concentrating on her face and arms.

For several years, Rudolf Nureyev in effect took over the company, as well as the leading roles of ballets he had created, for seasons at the Coliseum. In addition, he sometimes danced with the Ballet-Théâtre de Nancy, with a season adjoining the London Festival Ballet season.

Fokine's Le Spectre de la rose, *with Nureyev in the title role and Alexandra Wells as the Young Girl. Ballet Théâtre Français de Nancy, Edinburgh Festival, 1987.*

Christopher Bruce's The World Again, *with Janette Mulligan in the leading role. The curve of her body, supported by Martyn Fleming, suggests sadness and declining strength. London Festival Ballet, 1986.*

Peter Schaufuss took over from John Field as artistic director in 1984, and put his mark on the company by bringing in a number of dancers from other Common Market countries and by commissioning from Natalia Makarova a production of Act IV of *La Bayadère*. The remarkable event of 1986 was the creation of a ballet by Christopher Bruce, who as a dancer and choreographer had played a crucial role in the transformation of the Ballet Rambert two decades earlier. *The World Again* had a very strange theme of a woman suffering deeply and then dying – to be reborn on what seemed to be a different planet, where she could find happiness. Until cast in this role Janette Mulligan, the Australian artist who had become the leading ballerina in the company, had seemed a hard-working, well-trained dancer; now, rehearsed by Bruce, she emerged as a remarkable artist, able to pour deep feeling into her dance-images while retaining a fine restraint.

CHAPTER ELEVEN

The Ballets Russes Companies

Two Ballets Russes companies did much to spread a love of ballet around the world after the dissolution of the Diaghilev and Pavlova companies. Both retained a strongly Russian character: although they gradually took on more and more non-Russian dancers, their repertoires were largely derived from that of Diaghilev's company, and the choreographers were usually Russian or had Russian ancestry.

When the first Ballets Russes company was founded in 1932 by the Parisian impresario René Blum and the Russian impresario, Colonel W. de Basil, its quality derived almost entirely from the good taste and vision of Blum; de Basil was a tough-minded go-getter who, before long, succeeded in pushing out Blum. The company gained much, however, from the continuing work of Serge Grigoriev, who had also been Diaghilev's *régisseur*, and from the teaching and miming of Grigoriev's wife Lyubov Tchernicheva (who had been a leading Diaghilev dancer). The supreme dancer in the company was Alexandra Danilova, but there were also the three 'baby ballerinas' – Irina Baronova, Tamara Toumanova and Tatiana Riabouchinska – all born of Russian parents and trained in Paris by Preobrazhenskaya or Kshessinskaya. (Baronova and Toumanova were 13 when they joined the company; Riabouchinska was two years older.) Also trained by Preobrazhenskaya was the somewhat older ballerina Nina Verchinina (as were most of the *corps de ballet* dancers), and there were fine male soloists such as Leon Woizikowski, Yurek Shabelevsky and David Lichine.

Artistic policy was much influenced by Massine. He revived his Diaghilev ballets, and staged a new version of a frothy, charming ballet *Le Beau Danube* which he had created in 1924 for another company, and which had a leading role which permitted Danilova to show all her *demi-caractère* charm as a soubrette. The young Baronova had such extraordinary talent that she was able to make this role as provocative and sensual as the great Danilova had done.

However, every ballet company needs new ballets, and Massine provided these, creating a series of symphonic ballets that were possibly inspired by reports of Fyodor Lopukhov's *Tanzsymphonia*, staged in Petrograd in 1923 to Beethoven's Fourth Symphony. The form of a symphony is ill-adapted to ballet, and much of Massine's symphonic ballets looked pretentious, with unconvincing symbolism. But when he was able to use his flair for expressionism, the results were splendid. This happened in the slow movement of *Choreartium*, danced to Brahms' Symphony No. 4 in E minor. Here Massine skilfully adapted a tragic work by Isadora Duncan, *Funeral March*, using Nina Verchinina (who had been trained in German modern dance as well as in ballet) in the central role. The dragging steps, with bent-forward body – invented by Duncan for herself – looked magnificent when danced by Verchinina. *La Symphonie fantastique* of Berlioz already had a strong story line, and so lent itself quite well to dramatic choreography. This was easily the best of Massine's symphonic ballets, and he showed his talent superbly in the very expressionist 'March to the Scaffold', with a ferocious circle of judges who seemed to have stepped out of one of the prints by Daumier.

The first London season in 1933 was a triumph, extended for week after week, and from then on, the long London summer seasons were crucial to the company's survival. Before the arrival of the Ballets Russes company, the United States had

LEFT *Fokine's* Petrushka, *as danced by the de Basil Ballets Russes in the early 1930s, with superb performances by Yurek Shabelevsky (title role), Irina Baronova (Ballerina) and David Lichine (Blackamoor).*

seen little of good ballet, and it took longer for the company to establish itself there. However, it became more and more popular, performing one-night stands across the continent, and continuing Pavlova's work of spreading a love of ballet. In 1937, Blum founded another Ballets Russes company, luring away Massine. De Basil fought back by obtaining the services of Fokine. The following year, there was great excitement when both companies appeared in London simultaneously, with complementary repertoires. But the standards of neither company were as high as those of the original Ballets Russes de Monte Carlo. The de Basil company finally disbanded in 1952.

The other company, now directed by Massine and Sergei Denham, kept up the de Basil tradition of performing one-night stands across America – suggesting that ballet was essentially Russian and exotic. More and more American dancers joined the company, until it became, in effect, the American Ballets Russes. By now, Massine's new ballets had lost their appeal; he left in 1942, and Denham took over. Denham was able to commission one remarkable new American ballet from Agnes de Mille, *Rodeo*, with music by Aaron Copland and de Mille herself in the leading female role. The standard improved when Balanchine joined the company in 1944 and staged a number of abstract ballets. However, like the de Basil company, the Denham company eventually ran out of steam, disbanding in 1962.

LEFT Les Sylphides *(with choreography by Fokine) soon after the rise of the curtain. De Basil Ballets Russes, c. 1937.*
RIGHT Rodeo, *with which Agnes de Mille made a striking impact when she created it for the Denham Ballet Russe. (L to r) Casimir Kokic, De Mille, Frederick Franklin. Metropolitan Opera House, 1942.*

CHAPTER TWELVE

The Rise of Modern Dance

A very early solo created and danced by Isadora Duncan before leaving for Europe, Omar Made into Dance. *This dance illustrated verses from* The Rubaiyat, *during a lecture on Omar Khayam. Carnegie Hall Music Room, New York, 1898.*

In some ways, the rise of modern dance – stimulated by the research and theories of forward-looking pioneers long before great modern dancers emerged – was strangely like the rise of ballet as a self-sufficient art, 200 years earlier.

The first of these pioneers was François Delsarte (1811–71), a French music teacher who analysed the movements of the human body and devised a system for teaching the control of bodily movement. Delsartism came to be widely taught in the United States, and it stimulated the first two great modern dancers – Isadora Duncan and Ruth St Denis – to break away from ballet early in the 20th century and establish a new, free, barefoot kind of dancing. Isadora Duncan perfected her art in Europe, and mainly worked there; Ruth St Denis remained in America, where she worked first as a solo dancer, then joined with Ted Shawn to found Denishawn (both a school and a company) in Los Angeles in 1916.

The second progenitor of modern dance was the Vienna-born Emile Jaques-Dalcroze (1865–1950) who, like Delsarte, was a music teacher and theoretician with a passion for body movement. Working in Switzerland, Germany and Austria, he devised a system for developing musical sensibility through the translation of musical rhythms, phrasing and counterpoint into physical movements. Also like Delsarte, he avoided using the word 'dance' in connection with his teachings, but he had great influence on ballet. One of his favourite pupils, Marie Rambert, left him to collaborate with Nijinsky, but he made his mark on modern dance chiefly through two other pupils: the German Mary Wigman and the Czech-Austrian Rosalia Chladek.

A third influential theoretician was Bratislava-born Rudolf von Laban (1879–1958), who developed the use of space in dance. His teaching helped both Mary Wigman and Kurt Jooss to shape their choreographic and pedagogic ideas.

In Germany, modern dance took off despite – or rather because of – the terrible aftermath of the First World War, when there was boundless inflation and much starvation. Expressionism flourished in all the arts – and the most violently expressionistic of all the German barefoot dancers was the great artist Mary Wigman, performing on her own or with the backing of a chorus of dancers trained by her. The most powerful of all her solo creations was *Hexentanz* (*Witch Dance*), in which she wore a mask derived from her own face, but stylized to suggest the demonic character she incarnated. Her movements, with powerful rhythms and a menacing quality, took the form of starkly expressionistic dance-images. Fortunately, this dance has been preserved on film, so that we can still appreciate the power of her dancing at its best.

When she danced with a group, she was able to tackle more complex themes, but she was always the central figure, with the other dancers used in solid blocks, as a chorus. Nevertheless, she used two solo figures in *The Dance of Death*: Death himself was a barbaric, beast-like creature, forcing a chorus of dead people to rise from their graves and dance; and Wigman was a strange figure standing between the death figure and the group of dancers. Once again, all the dancers wore masks, so that they appeared as symbolic figures.

The music for this work – all percussion – was played partly by the composer, and partly by the dancers themselves. This fusion of percussion and dancing was to become a typical feature of

Mary Wigman in one of her most powerful solos, Schicksalslied (Song of Fate)*. The boldly stylized, expressionist hands are characteristic of her work. From the* Tanzgesänge *cycle, 1935. Presumably the photographer retouched the photo, making the eyeballs frighteningly white.*

German *Ausdruckstanz*. Out of her dances, Wigman established a technique, and this was taught to students in her many schools all over Germany. The best of her pupils, such as Harald Kreutzberg, Palucca and Hanya Holm, established themselves as solo performers and/or dancer-choreographers leading a group, but Wigman continued to stand out as a giant. No one could equal her in the projection of demonic forces.

Kurt Jooss differed from Wigman in being strongly influenced by ballet, and in working in close collaboration with a remarkable teacher, Sigurd Leeder. Remaining strongly imbued with German *Ausdruckstanz* ideals, they adopted only certain aspects of ballet. However, Jooss was greatly impressed by the ballets performed by the Diaghilev company, and staged his own versions of a number of them, including *Petrushka*, *The Prodigal Son* and *Pulcinella*. The Jooss dancers, unlike those trained by Wigman, wore shoes – though these were not blocked.

By 1932, Jooss was ready to create his masterpiece, *The Green Table*. He took inspiration from old wood-cuts showing the dance of death, but gave his ballet a strong contemporary flavour. The portrayal of the diplomats around the green table, with hypocritically polite hand gestures, was superbly satirical – and given extra horror by the satirical half-masks they wore. Then came a series of scenes in a more balletic style, showing the horrors of war. Each time a character died, the dreadful figure of Death, in a costume suggesting a skeleton and wearing make-up suggesting a skull, came on stage to lead away the dead person – appearing each time in a different mood. The profiteer was treated in a strongly satirical fashion, whereas the partisan woman who killed a soldier was shown sympathetically.

This ballet won a prize in Paris, and established Jooss as a choreographer of international calibre; indeed, *The Green Table* is now successfully performed by ballet companies in numerous countries.

In Austria, the outstanding pioneer of modern dance was Rosalia Chladek – who was born in Brno, trained at Dalcroze's school at Hellerau near Dresden (1921–24), and became one of the leading recital dancers in Germany and Austria. During the Thirties she was artistic director of the Hellerau–Laxenburg School (which had moved to Laxenburg near Vienna) and developed further her own technique and style of modern dance, which was much less expressionistic than Wigman's. While modern dance almost disappeared in Germany after the Second World War, Chladek continued to be honoured and influential as a teacher/choreographer in Vienna during the post-war years.

Modern dance was established in Britain in 1930 at Dartington Hall, near Totnes in Devon, by the talented Australian dancer and choreographer Margaret Barr, who had trained with Martha Graham in America. Her Dance-Drama Group – which included the fine dramatic dancer Teda de Moore from South Africa, and enjoyed the collaboration of Edmund Rubbra as composer and Peter Goffin as designer – created a series of dramatic works for performance in the Barn Theatre at Dartington, the finest of which was Barr's *The Three Sisters*. The Ballets Jooss, forced to leave Germany in 1933 after Hitler took power, also took up residence at Dartington Hall, but spent half of each year on tour.

In the United States, modern dance initially developed more slowly than in Germany and

LEFT *Rehearsal photo (1935) of Kurt Jooss's* The Green Table, *with cynical Gentlemen in Black in conference. They wear half-masks, so both male and female members of the Jooss company participate.*
RIGHT *This close-up of Martha Graham in her solo* Lamentation *(1930) gives a vivid suggestion of the powerful projection and originality of her dance-images.*

Austria. The Denishawn Company, led by Ruth St Denis and Ted Shawn, danced exotic pieces, suggesting East Indian, Amerindian, Aztec and other styles. The main technique that they taught was, however, a simplified form of ballet.

Martha Graham broke away from Denishawn in 1923, and worked hard to create a style of her own, tackling very different themes from the exotic ones favoured by Denishawn. Influenced by photographs and descriptions of Wigman's dancing, she abandoned the simplified ballet technique taught to Denishawn dancers and began to develop her own technique from the stark angular movements (with much use of the floor) which she choreographed for herself and a group of female dancers she had trained and used as a chorus. Her extraordinary originality emerged clearly in *Lamentation*, a solo created in 1930. Dressed in stretch fabric that extended down from her arms to her legs, keeping her torso hidden unless she twisted round, she created extraordinary dance-images, unlike any seen before. This costume showed her imagination, skill and originality as a designer; she experimented with the costumes on other dancers before finalizing them, making sure that they flowed with the dancing and did not trip them up.

Her own style, and her own approach to dance, were clearly established before Wigman came to the United States for the first time in 1930. By this time, Graham was one of a group of American dancer/choreographers working in New York – going to each other's concerts (each of which were performed after many months of work) and taking stimulus from them – but she was the most advanced artistically. She retained this leading position for decade after decade, continuing to be creative and to tour with her company, watching every performance from the wings and giving corrections – even after she had passed the age of 90. No other dancer/choreographer has had such a long creative career.

Of the 250-odd works created by Graham over half a century, a certain number stand out because of their power and stark individuality. Her studies of the dancing of the Indians in New Mexico –

Martha Graham, as the Virgin, dancing the central role in her austere, ritualistic piece Primitive Mysteries *(1931). The stylized hand positions often recurred in later pieces.*

with its strange fusion of Indian and Christian traditions – inspired her to create two works in very different styles: *Primitive Mysteries* (1931) and *El Penitente* (1940). *Frontier* (1935) and *Appalachian Spring* (1944) showed her deep feeling for the spirit of the frontier. *Night Journey* (1947) showed her tackling an ancient Greek myth in her own way – presenting the mythical story of Oedipus as seen by Jocasta, and coming boldly to terms with the sexual implications of the myth and fusing this with the sexual conflicts of a modern woman. This was only one of a number of works she based on Greek myths.

In *Diversion of Angels* (1948), she showed that her expressionist technique of emphasizing contractions and releases could project the happiness of young love. In *Letter to the World* (1940), she gave her own interpretation of the life and poetry of Emily Dickinson, while in *Seraphic Dialogue* (1955), she presented, in a very ritualistic way, the life of Joan of Arc, transmuted into a myth. She created a marvellously amusing satire of herself in *Acrobats of God* (1960) – with a cruel ringmaster (brilliantly danced by David Wood) driving her to create. At first, she took the leading role in nearly all her works, while continuing to train fine artists. After she ceased to dance, she created works with others in the leading roles, as well as restaging earlier masterworks with others taking her roles. Hers was a career without parallel in the history of theatrical dance.

Her creativity had its roots in the violent contradictions within her nature – contradictions which remained alive and kicking throughout her life, thus enabling her to keep renewing herself and remaining active as a choreographer into her nineties. Although she was very American – having descended from ten generations of New Englanders – she was strongly drawn to the East, and in the final stages of her career, two of her leading dancers – the supremely gifted Takako Asakawa and Yuriko Nimura – were Japanese.

No other American dancer/choreographer has been as influential as she was – indeed, her technique is now taught all around the world. However, while Graham was flourishing, there was a marvellous flowering of other American artists who took their own paths, and even those who worked with Graham for a time tended to move off in new directions. Together, they established American modern/contemporary dance as a major contribution to world culture.

Two other major dancer/choreographers started their careers at the same time and place as Martha Graham – at the Denishawn School in Los Angeles. However, Doris Humphrey and Charles Weidman stayed much longer; indeed, Humphrey had begun to create 'music-visualization' pieces for the company before she and Weidman left in 1928.

They made a good team, although they differed very much in temperament and outlook. Determined to establish dance as an independent art, Humphrey created a number of works without music, but she was above all interested in form, and showed this very clearly in one of her most famous pieces, *Air on a G String*, with five cloaked dancers stepping out in formal patterns, and causing their cloaks to intertwine. Her fascination with form found ideal expression in *The Shakers* (1931), in which she used strict patterns to suggest the austerity of the lives of this religious community, but had the dance-images imbued with ecstatic feeling. Weidman, in contrast, was much concerned with drama, satire and mimed humour: *Lynch Town* showed onlookers at a lynching moving with frenzy along a dramatic diagonal, in a path of light. His fables were quite different in style: in *The Unicorn in the Garden* he brought together the text written by the humorist James Thurber and brilliantly stylized mime that caught exactly the ironical flavour of the words.

The Mexican-born José Limón, trained by Humphrey, formed a company with her as artistic director in 1946. His finest work was *The Moor's Pavane* (1949), in which he treated the story of Shakespeare's *Othello* in a very stylized way – as a pavane (a stately dance) – but caused the stark emotions to well up through the formal musical patterns. This work has been added to the repertoires of a number of ballet companies.

Merce Cunningham had training in the Graham technique in Seattle, and danced in the Graham company – as a leading artist – from 1940 to 1945. Then he broke away and, like Graham, established a very individual style of his own, as well as a company. Absorbing influences from ballet, he developed a style in which the body could move in any direction at any moment. All

Doris Humphrey with dancers of the Humphrey-Weidman Company in her piece The Shakers *(*Dance of the Chosen*), inspired by prints of a sect expressing religious fervour in ceremonial dances (1930).*

his works were abstract, and under the influence of his friend, the composer John Cage, he took care that none of the elements in his works – dance, music, costumes, scenery and lighting – had any connection with the others. Such was the quality of his dancing at the centre of his works – and also, for twenty years, the dancing of the glorious artist Carolyn Brown, trained in ballet by Tudor – that he succeeded in making strange works such as *Variations V* (1965) and *Suite by Chance* (in which the combination of elements was determined by the tossing of a coin) oddly compelling. When he developed arthritis in both feet, and could only hobble, he still continued to dance, and even to give solo recitals – dancing mainly with his arms. He likes to dance in gymnasiums, where he presents 'Events': fragments of choreography extracted from a number of his works, and accompanied by improvised music. Here his art is seen at its most fascinating and varied: the fragments hang together amazingly well.

Lester Horton, working in Los Angeles completely independently of the artists based in New York, developed his own style of choreography and his own technique – although he had guest teachers who taught German modern dance in the Wigman style, and he read avidly about the happenings in New York. He tackled a wide variety of themes – ranging from *Salome* and *The Rite of Spring* to his Mexican epic *Conquest*. His technique continued to develop out of his choreography, in the usual modern-dance manner, but he also took ideas from the dances of the Plains Indians. The highly talented Alvin Ailey took the Horton technique to New York after the latter's death in 1953, and there formed a splendid company of black dancers, the Alvin Ailey American Dance Theater. His masterpiece, *Revelations*, was based on Negro spirituals and his memories of baptisms in a river in his native Texas; the spirituals come to life in all their fervour in the gloriously expressive dance-images he created, especially when danced by Judith Jamison. *Revelations* has remained at the centre of the Ailey repertoire.

Paul Taylor – although trained in ballet by Tudor and deeply influenced by him – went on to dance with the Graham company, and then developed his own highly individual approach to modern dance. He is marvellously versatile, tack-

TOP Fabrications, *with Merce Cunningham (right) dancing with his company. With only partial use of both feet, he still dominated the stage with compelling arm and head movements.*
RIGHT *Alvin Ailey's masterpiece* Revelations, *danced by his company. The complex patterns formed by the dancers – part of a flux of lyrical movement – show Ailey's acute sense of form.*
OPPOSITE TOP *Paul Taylor's* Aureole, *performed by London Festival Ballet, c. 1970 – with the ballet dancers in bare feet tackling American modern dance with gusto.*

ling a wide variety of themes in a great range of styles, intensely musical and sometimes very humorous. His funniest works are *Three Epitaphs* (1956 – in which the dancers, wearing costumes covered in small mirrors reflecting the spotlights, make odd little movements) and *Party Mix* (with grotesque juxtapositions of dancers). His most ambitious piece, and his first full-length work, is *Orbs* (1966), danced to three late string quartets by Beethoven: planets moving around the sun are used as a metaphor for human society. His most balletic work is the abstract *Aureole* (1962 – Nureyev has delighted in dancing in this), and perhaps his strangest is *Private Domain*, with the front of the stage covered by strips of cloth, so that different spectators see different choreography.

After establishing herself in America in 1931, the Wigman-trained teacher and choreographer Hanya Holm evolved her own distinctive fusion of German and American modern dance. Alwin Nikolais, after years as Holm's associate, became a master of total theatre, creating the music (on a synthesizer), the lighting and the slide projections at the same time as the choreography. His most magical work is *Tent* (1968). In this, a huge cloth is suspended by cables, which are adjusted so that it takes many different shapes; on to these are thrown colourful and mysterious abstract patterns from ten slide projectors. Although he claims that *Tent* is abstract, like his other works, it clearly has an ambitious theme: the origins of the universe and the progress of humanity from the Garden of Eden to the violent world of today.

Anna Sokolow stands out from other American modern-dance choreographers in that – although she trained with Graham, and danced in her company from 1930 to 1939 – she had her own independent company for some years in the Thirties, and developed her own approach to choreography, with a stress on isolation and despair. Originally trained in ballet herself, she remained just as happy working with ballet dancers, and those trained in both ballet and modern, as with solely modern dancers. She spent some years in Mexico, establishing modern dance there and developing her keen sense of rhythm in contact with complex Latin American rhythms.

Becoming a freelance choreographer, she

LEFT *No photo can catch the magic of Alwin Nikolais's* Tent, *with its complex use of multiple projections; he used cables to change the symbolism of the 'tent'.*
RIGHT Shizen, *created for Pilobolus in 1973, with choreography by Moses Pendleton and Alison Chase. Performed by Pendleton and Cynthia Quinn for Momix.*

BELOW *Glen Tetley's masterpiece* Pierrot Lunaire, *with Pierrot (Mark Baldwin) hanging from the scaffolding tower. Staged by Tetley for Ballet Rambert in 1967.*

staged her works for many companies around the world. Her strong feeling for despair and isolation emerged with particular clarity in *Rooms*, staged for numerous companies. In it, four men and four women each have their own chair, symbolizing the lonely space in which they live in a big city, and each reacts to loneliness in a different way. The actions of the suicidal girl are very strange: standing on her chair, she seems to look towards death with exaltation.

Glen Tetley is another highly talented American choreographer who formed his own company to establish himself, later becoming a freelance choreographer, and merging the traditions of modern dance and ballet in a new way. His very first work, *Pierrot Lunaire* (1962), in which he treated the *commedia dell'arte* figures of Pierrot, Columbine and Brighella in a complex and very individual way, remains his masterpiece. This ballet, and later fine pieces such as *Mythical Hunters*, did much to help the Netherlands Dance Theatre, the reorganized Ballet Rambert and the Batsheva Dance Company in Israel to establish themselves as companies with distinct personalities.

Pilobolus, founded in 1971 by Moses Pendleton and Jonathan Wolken, established its own style, drawing upon the flair of its two founder-members for many kinds of sport. The dances were choreographed by the dancers themselves, and included very strange images. One of its most extraordinary achievements was *Shizen*, devised and danced by Moses Pendleton and Alison

Chase. This was inspired by the sound of the Japanese *shakuhachi* flute, which is closely associated with Zen, and the dancing had a Zen quality. Many of the dance-images suggested a maple leaf floating down to settle on water, a central metaphor in Zen: it implies nature as a whole, and the harmony of the forces of the universe. Though the dance lasted 18 minutes, and remained slow, it never lost its tight grip on audiences. With hands over faces, the gently swaying dancers suggested a tree; arms trailing from side to side suggested flowing water; and when Pendleton picked up his partner and caused her horizontal body to sway, the two bodies combined to suggest a falling leaf. Here was dancing totally remote from expressionism; indeed, the dance created an atmosphere rather like the mysterious dances of Birgit Åkesson, a great Swedish modern dancer who established her own style and approach several decades earlier.

RIGHT *The mysterious death figures in* Ghost Dances, *with choreography and setting by Christopher Bruce. Ballet Rambert, 1981.*
BELOW *Dancing the lead in his own piece* Liquid Assets, *the gifted American artist Tom Jobe moves with eye-catching ease and quirky accents. London Contemporary Dance Theatre, 1982.*

In Britain during the war, modern dance became much more widely known than before through the touring of the Ballets Jooss, with government support; a number of English ballet-trained dancers joined it, and did well. But Jooss had exhausted his capacity for choreographic development, and disbanded the company in 1947. In 1949, he returned to Germany, and re-established his company in Essen for a time; from then on, his main work was the supervision of revivals of *The Green Table* and another fine Jooss ballet *Big City* (1932), for various ballet companies around the world. This work was taken over after Kurt Jooss's death by his daughter Anna Markard.

Modern dance returned to the stage in Britain in 1966 when the assistant director of Ballet Rambert, Norman Morrice (much influenced by his studies in the Martha Graham School in New York, in 1961–62), transformed the Ballet Rambert. He reduced its size until it was much smaller, and then stressed modern dance, even though ballet training was continued in the company classes. Morrice was able to build up a fine

repertoire of a new type, with dancers coming to maturity in challenging works (fusing modern dance and ballet) by Anna Sokolow (*Deserts*) and Glen Tetley (*Pierrot Lunaire*, *Mythical Hunters*, *Embrace Tiger and Return to Mountain*). Tetley created the last work specifically for Ballet Rambert, drawing on the Chinese ritual dance-form *T'ai chi chuan*. Almost the whole of the company's former ballet repertoire, including the Tudor masterpieces, was scrapped, except for the Nijinsky ballet *L'Après-midi d'un faune* – which was revived with the help of an amateur film of a 1931 performance – and Tudor's 1937 *Dark Elegies*.

Christopher Bruce survived the reorganization of the company with *élan*. He danced superbly in the title role of *Pierrot Lunaire*. Then he developed as a choreographer, influenced first by Tudor and Tetley and then by the Czech choreographer Jiří Kylián. Bruce's masterpiece for the Ballet Rambert was *Ghost Dances*, showing the oppression of Indians in South America and their very strange attitude towards death.

Thanks to the work of Robert Cohan (who had been a leading dancer in the Martha Graham company for many years), training in contemporary dance – a term that, in recent years, Graham-trained dancers have come to prefer to 'modern dance' – has been firmly established in Britain, primarily through the London Contemporary Dance School, directed by Cohan, which turns out a number of dancers every year. However, as only a few can hope to be accepted into the London Contemporary Dance Theatre (founded in 1969), graduates from the School have been joining together to form small dance groups in which they can try out their own ideas.

In 1989 Robert Cohan was succeeded as director of the LCDT by the American, Dan Wagoner.

For a time, Tom Jobe, a witty, impudent, highly individual dancer/choreographer from Texas, made his presence strongly felt in performances by the London Contemporary Dance Theatre – above all when he danced in his own work *Liquid Assets* (1982). Here was jazz-dancing with a difference. After leaving LCDT he returned to create sparkling works for the company –*Run Like Thunder* (1983) and *Rite Electrik* (1984) and sections of *Phantasmagoria* (1987) – but no one could replace Tom Jobe the dancer.

CHAPTER THIRTEEN

American Ballet

In the United States in the first half of the 20th century, creative artists who in Britain would have entered the ballet world found it natural to move into modern dance. For many years, Americans thought of ballet as an exotic art imported from Russia. (Indeed, the word 'ballet' was then used by the modern dancers as a term of abuse.) As a consequence, the first outstanding American ballets were staged much later than British ones had been, and they came into existence only after superb British and Russian ballets had been brought together in the repertoire of the first great American company, Ballet Theatre.

This was founded in 1939, when the highly imaginative Richard Pleasant persuaded the wealthy American dancer Lucia Chase to found a large company bringing together the best existing ballets, staged if possible by their creators, and a large number of talented dancers. For a few crucial years, Pleasant established himself as a creative artistic director, although he lacked the professional expertise of Durazzo, Diaghilev and Rambert. Nothing less than the best would do: Fokine, Nijinska and Tudor all rehearsed their own ballets, Dolin rehearsed the classics, and Eugene Loring was *régisseur* of the American wing – with provision for new ballets by the very promising Agnes de Mille. Pleasant even instituted a Negro wing and a Spanish wing, and planned an American modern-dance wing – thus showing himself well ahead of his time. Even so, his visionary project resulted in the creation of a great ballet company of a new kind with limitless possibilities for development.

Notwithstanding numerous flaws in the execution of Pleasant's ideas, the company was a great success. Although the new American ballets were at a very different level from the imported ones, and many of the American dancers (later to develop into great artists, through maturing within the company) were not ready for the subtlety of performance required of them, audiences responded well. In fact, Ballet Theatre was very American in its complex diversity: the company could have come into existence in no other country.

Tudor's influence on Ballet Theatre soon became dominant, and as he revived his London ballets, he fostered the development of a number of great dancers. By 1942, he was ready to create a major new ballet, one that he had had no time to stage with his own company in London. This was *Pillar of Fire*, with the great dramatic dancer Nora Kaye taking the challenging central role of Hagar. This woman, who believes that her beloved prefers her younger sister, hardly ever leaves the stage: we see everything through her eyes.

Hagar (Nora Kaye) in a torment of conflict – helplessly attracted to, yet repelled by, a man projecting vulgar machismo *(Hugh Laing). Antony Tudor's* Pillar of Fire, *Ballet Theatre, 1942.*

In Antony Tudor's Undertow *Medusa (Diana Adams) drives the Transgressor (Hugh Laing) to murder by seducing him with her powerful sexuality. Ballet Theatre, 1945.*

Tudor, using music one would have thought totally unsuited to ballet – Schönberg's *Verklärte Nacht* (*Transfigured Night*) – achieved something quite new in dramatic ballet: he presented layer upon layer of feeling, and great depth of characterization, via dance-images of extraordinary power and originality. He gave the important role of the Young Man from the House Opposite to Hugh Laing, an outstanding male dancer who had come with him from London. Laing was Tudor's closest friend – understanding him better than anyone – and projected the character of the man to whom Hagar succumbs in despair, the epitome of male arrogance, sexuality and insensitivity. Tudor himself danced the very demanding and subtle role of the man with whom Hagar is in love, but with whom she can make no contact because of her Victorian inhibitions. Small groups of *corps de ballet* dancers were used in a new way: as human beings, but also as projections of Hagar's internal conflicts. Indeed, the triumphant first night of *Pillar of Fire* was a crucial one in the development of American ballet.

Tudor followed this masterpiece with other outstanding ballets – notably a one-act version of *Romeo and Juliet*. (Although he liked the Prokofiev score, he found that, if he used it, the ballet would be much too long, so he used music by Frederick Delius.) Another work of immense power was *Undertow*, in which the treatment of psychological conflict was even more complex than in *Pillar of Fire*. Hugh Laing did wonders with the central role of an idealistic adolescent, driven to murder because everything he encounters turns out to be a fake, who is seduced by a woman of overpowering sexuality (Nora Kaye).

Jerome Robbins (who joined Ballet Theatre in order to dance in Tudor's immensely challenging and stimulating ballet *Dark Elegies*) began a remarkable creative career with *Fancy Free* (1944), the girl-chasing adventures of three sailors on shore leave. Nothing like *Fancy Free* had ever been seen before: although constructed with extraordinary precision, the dancers interpreted their roles with the greatest ease and spontaneity.

Agnes de Mille was not as fortunate. Accustomed to dancing her own choreography while coming to maturity in London, partnered by Hugh Laing, she was artistically crippled when creating ballets for Ballet Theatre because she was not allowed to dance in them. However, while working for the Ballets Russes de Monte Carlo, she

As a choreographer, Jerome Robbins showed mastery in putting contemporary American life into ballet. In his ballet Fancy Free *he makes friends with Janet Reed. Ballet Theatre, 1944.* RIGHT *George Balanchine rehearsing a young dancer. New York City Ballet, 1965.*

created a delightful cowboy ballet *Rodeo*, with herself in the lead, and this fine American work was then added to the Ballet Theatre repertoire.

The company made a tremendous impact when it performed at Covent Garden in 1946: nothing remotely like this repertoire had ever been seen in London, and the season had to be extended for two weeks. However, then the company began to degenerate as, one by one, its finest dancers, tired of constant touring, left it. In 1950, Tudor, too, found it necessary to leave, taking with him three dancers who had matured superbly in his ballets: Nora Kaye, Hugh Laing and Diana Adams. He hoped to continue his creative career within the New York City Ballet, but this proved impossible; that company was much too tightly geared to the ballets of George Balanchine. The result was that Tudor abandoned choreography for many years, and concentrated on teaching.

The New York City Ballet, formed in 1948, was very fortunate in that it had a regular home in New York – first, the New York City Center, and then the New York State Theater at Lincoln Center. Unlike the dancers of Ballet Theatre, the NYCB's dancers could take class every day, and live at home – instead of remaining constantly on tour.

With his loyal friend Lincoln Kirstein taking over administration, Balanchine was able to work with complete artistic freedom, using dancers trained at the School of American Ballet and able to give him exactly what he needed as a choreographer. In many ways, he was like Petipa, creating a steady stream of ballets with no apparent difficulty. He was a round peg in a round hole: the company needed a flow of new ballets, to keep up the interest of critics and the public, and Balanchine responded with ease and assurance to this demand, creating dozens of primarily abstract ballets. He was well aware of his affinity to Petipa; indeed, he said that much of his choreography was derived from ballets by Petipa which he remembered from his youth in Russia, but which were unknown in the outside world. Unlike Petipa, however, he was able to use first-class music whenever he chose; he even said – with typical irony – that if people were bored by his ballets they could close their eyes and listen to the music. In fact, people were not bored by his ballets: they learned to relish his quirky, very individual use of music – sometimes, as he composed his *enchaînements*, taking little account of what the composer was 'saying'.

As Ballet Theatre – later called American Ballet Theatre – declined in quality, and rarely visited New York, Balanchine became more and more of a dominant figure in American ballet, acquiring a status comparable to that of Petipa. In fact, one might call the period 1950–80 the Balanchine era in American ballet. Even after his death, his influence remained overwhelming: nearly all the aspiring young American choreographers imitated him.

Strangely, Balanchine showed little interest in preserving the special qualities of his best ballets such as *Agon*. When creating this, he responded with sensitivity to the development of Stravinsky's music, in which the composer moved towards the advanced style of Anton von Webern. For the climax of the ballet, Balanchine constructed a *pas de deux* of fascinating ingenuity, in which the two

dancers keep some parts of their bodies in contact. (Here he was probably influenced by memories of the final scene of *Tanzsymphonia*, created by Fyodor Lopukhov in Petrograd in 1923, with Balanchine in the cast; in the final 'cosmogonic spiral' Lopukhov had all the dancers maintain contact with each other.)

Agon had such quality that it kept its place in the NYCB repertoire, but gradually it lost many of its nuances. Fortunately, Arthur Mitchell, the marvellous black classical dancer who created the male role in the *pas de deux*, remembered all the subtle touches that Balanchine had added to his original choreography, and restored these when he revived the ballet for his own great company, the Dance Theater of Harlem.

It was in 1934 that Balanchine, working with the students of the School of American Ballet, clearly established his own American type of abstract dance in *Serenade*. The shape of this ballet was partly determined by accident: the number of students attending the school at this time varied daily, and this determined the number of dancers he used for choreography on each day. The *enchaînements* became more complicated as the ballet went on, so he dropped from the later sections the dancers who could not cope with the choreography. He was much helped by the fact that he had chosen an episodic piece of music by Tchaikovsky – a composer with whom he felt deeply in harmony, partly because of the familiarity he had developed with the Tchaikovsky ballets in Russia. At one point, he added a strange little episode in mime that looked back to his Diaghilev ballets, in that it avoided any precise storyline. This work became the signature of the New York City Ballet, and has been constantly kept in its repertoire, as well as in those of many other companies around the world. It provided a model for the scores of abstract ballets that Balanchine created for the NYCB – although he never repeated his backward look at his Diaghilev days.

Strangely enough, one of the finest of all his ballets, *Theme and Variations*, was created not for his own company but for Ballet Theatre. The structure and style of the music – the final movement of Tchaikovsky's Suite No. 3 in G for Orchestra – was exactly suited to the type of *enchaînements* he delighted in. He was able to maintain a fine balance between female and male dancing because, at this time, Ballet Theatre had, as well as the fabulous ballerina Alicia Alonso, a number of fine male dancers, notably Igor Youskevitch.

Throughout his long, career, Balanchine found stimulus in taking in hand young and promising *danseuses* and moulding them into remarkable

artists. They also became his close companions for some years (in and out of wedlock), although his final inamorata, Suzanne Farrell, refused his proposal and married another man. One very unusual and delightful ballet that derived from his close association with one of his beloved prima ballerinas (and later wife), Tanaquil LeClercq, was *Bourrée fantasque*. Having great confidence in her individuality and creativity, he encouraged her to improvise her own choreography, and she poured delectable humour into her dancing.

Jerome Robbins created a number of sharply contrasted ballets for his own company, Ballets USA – including *Moves* (1959), danced in silence, but showing such musicality that it seemed to create its own silent music. In addition, he both directed and choreographed the musical *West Side Story*, bringing together the dancing, acting and singing so perfectly that this production seemed likely to lift the musical to a new artistic plane. (Regrettably, this did not happen.) During his first period with the New York City Ballet (1949–59), he created (1953) his own very personal version of *L'Après-midi d'un faune*, translating not only its title (as *Afternoon of a Faun*), but also,

ABOVE *George Balanchine perfected his abstract, neo-classical romanticism in* Serenade *(1934), in which almost all the dancing is feminine. ('Ballet is woman' – G.B.) Performed by New York City Ballet, 1969.*

imaginatively, the theme used by Nijinsky: two ballet dancers are practising, and even perform a *pas de deux* together, but remain immured in their private worlds. *The Concert* (1956) is a gorgeously satirical picture of an audience at a concert, moving more and more into fantasy – just as the Marx Brothers do in the best scenes of their best films. Rejoining the New York City Ballet, Robbins treated piano music by Chopin in a semi-abstract manner in *Dances at a Gathering* (1969) – revealing many moods, giving a hint of Polish national-dance steps, knitting together a wealth of solos, *pas de deux* and so on with subtle musicality, and finally suggesting people settling down in a new land of freedom, as his own parents had done.

After finding his way back to creativity in London in 1966–70, Antony Tudor rejoined the American Ballet Theatre in 1974. Previously, he had only returned at intervals to rehearse his ballets; now he became closely involved, and took advantage of the presence in the company of a magical young dancer, Gelsey Kirkland (who had left the New York City Ballet after vainly attempting to make herself into a replica of Balanchine's then-current muse, Suzanne Farrell) to create for Kirkland a masterly semi-abstract ballet with hints of Proust: *The Leaves Are Fading* (1975).

After the retirement of Lucia Chase in 1980, American Ballet Theatre was directed by an artist who had defected from the Kirov Ballet (formerly the Imperial Russian Ballet in St Petersburg) in the wake of Nureyev and Makarova. As a dancer, Mikhail Baryshnikov was superb, making the most difficult and unpredictable *enchaînements* look easy, but as the artistic director, he had to face problems that were fiendishly difficult.

A third major American company was formed by Robert Joffrey in 1954, its establishment being greatly helped by his friend Gerald Arpino, who contributed a stream of new ballets. Joffrey himself worked mainly as artistic director, constantly widening his repertoire by bringing in ballets of major choreographers of the past and present, such as Bournonville, Fokine, Massine, Tudor, Ashton and Robbins, together with two masterpieces from the world of modern dance: Jooss's *The Green Table* and Limón's *The Moor's Pavane*. Although Joffrey was not prolific like

BELOW *Tanaquil LeClerq danced with grace, style and elegance in Balanchine ballets – and her improvised humour in his* Bourrée Fantasque *was irresistible. New York City Ballet, 1949.*

LEFT *Tudor created a semi-abstract ballet of subtle moods in* The Leaves Are Fading, *building his ballet around the artistry of Gelsey Kirkland (partnered by Jonas Kåge). American Ballet Theatre, 1975.*
BELOW LEFT *In Robert Joffrey's* Astarte, *the love-goddess Astarte (Trinette Singleton) bewitches the young man (Maximilian Zomosa). City Center Joffrey Ballet, 1967.*
RIGHT *Mikhail Baryshnikov taking class. American Ballet Theatre, New York, 1984.*

Arpino, he was more original, and created some remarkable ballets for the repertoire – notably *Astarte* (1967).

This treated an ancient myth about the Phoenician love-goddess Astarte in quite a new way, with her male devotee in modern dress. The whole of the proscenium opening was filled in with a stretchable translucent gauze, pulled back into deep curves by cables. A set of four films, skilfully made by Gardner Compton, and projected from four synchronized projectors, threw huge moving images of the two solo dancers on to this gauze, with the 'live' dancers usually visible behind it. Since the images were projected on to a curving surface, they were distorted in a mysterious way, and at times, images from more than one camera were superimposed – thus adding to the strange effect. Moreover, the big filmed images combined very strangely with the dance-images of the much smaller 'live' performers on stage. At the beginning and end of the ballet, a filmed image of the hero – walking into the theatre from the street, and finally walking out again – combined neatly with the movements of the 'live' dancers in the theatre. Visually, the total effect was highly impressive; regrettably, the ballet could only be revived with difficulty, for every time the cast changed, the films had to be reshot.

It was typical of Joffrey – with his receptiveness to new ideas – that in 1987, after establishing a second centre in Los Angeles, he should commission a revival of great artistic importance: Nijinsky's original version of *Le Sacre du printemps*. Even as a child, Joffrey had been fascinated with Nijinsky, feeling a closeness with this extraordinary artist, and he was able to find out a great deal about him from his teacher Alexandra Federovna, who had danced with Nijinsky. In 1955, he learned even more from Marie Rambert.

When the ballet historian Millicent Hodson came to Joffrey with a project for reconstructing *Le Sacre*, he jumped at the idea. Hodson gathered together every scrap of surviving evidence about Nijinsky's choreography, including descriptions by eye witnesses, drawings and Rambert's notes

ABOVE *Nijinsky's* The Rite of Spring, *as reconstructed by Millicent Hodson for Joffrey Ballet, 1987. (L to r) Meg Gurin, Julie Janus, Jill Davidson. Resemblances to photos of the original ballet are manifest.*
TOP RIGHT *Dancers of Dance Theater of Harlem pouring virility, vitality, spontaneity, individuality and humour into* Troy Games, *created by American-born Robert North for London Contemporary Dance Theatre.*
RIGHT *The death of Giselle (Virginia Johnson) at the end of Act I, in Arthur Mitchell's superbly detailed transposition of the ballet to Louisiana. Dance Theatre of Harlem, 1986.*

on the score. The sets and costumes designed by Roerich were reconstructed by the Roerich specialist Kenneth Archer, who also had to search the archives for evidence.

Naturally, the reconstruction could not claim to be identical to the original: that was impossible. However, Millicent Hodson avoided imposing any dance-image which clashed with the evidence, and the result on stage had a mysterious quality unlike that of any other ballet. Indeed, the reconstruction represented a major addition to the company's repertoire and did much to lift a crucially important 20th-century ballet from pre-history into history. It is a lasting tribute to Robert Joffrey who, sadly, died in March 1988 at the age of 57.

Arthur Mitchell, the black artist who became a leading classical dancer in the New York City Ballet, founded the Dance Theater of Harlem following the assassination of Dr Martin Luther King in 1968, to give opportunities to black dancers who, although welcome in modern dance companies, had great difficulty in joining classical ballet companies. Even though the influence of Balanchine on Mitchell was clear, the DTH dancers brought their own individuality to all their roles. This happened in Balanchine ballets and also in a fine variety of other ballets, some of them establishing links with black traditions of dance – notably Geoffrey Holder's *Dougla*, with roots in Jamaica. Arthur Mitchell's supreme achievement was to stage a version of *Giselle* which placed it among black slaves in Louisiana at exactly the time the ballet was created. The slave society of the period showed astonishing affinities with the life shown in the original ballet – wealthy slaves, dressed with the utmost elegance, owned slaves of their own – and Mitchell was able to show an exact parallel with the traditional interaction of a nobleman in disguise and a simple village maiden. Even Giselle's grave was changed, in an authentic way: the ground outside New Orleans is so waterlogged that tombs must be above ground, and the DTH version of Giselle's tomb reflected this. Virginia Johnson gave a marvellously fresh and spontaneous interpretation of Giselle, and all the dancers showed a remarkable flair for classical dancing in the romantic style of the period.

CHAPTER FOURTEEN

Soviet Ballet

After the 1917 revolution, ballet inside the Soviet Union was in danger of losing all its traditions, and even of being destroyed completely. It had, after all, been the Imperial Russian Ballet, paid for out of the privy purse of the Tsar, and could have been attacked as having no interest for the masses.

Fortunately, however, Anatoly Lunacharsky, the first Commissar for Education – who also had control of all theatrical arts – was an erudite man who, before the war, had been a professional critic of theatre, art and music, and had written about the Paris seasons of the Diaghilev Ballet in 1912–13. In speech after speech, he defended the preservation of balletic traditions, and stated with firmness that ballet would not be abolished in the Soviet Union. Thanks to this great man – who invited Isadora Duncan to perform in the Soviet Union and represented a Soviet equivalent of Durazzo – the great Petrograd (later Leningrad) company preserved much of its repertoire, and continued to train fine dancers in its school.

The director of the ballet company, Fyodor Lopukhov (brother of the Diaghilev ballerina, Lydia Lopokova) was a gifted and forward-looking choreographer who created ballets that challenged comparison with the best that were being produced by the Ballets Russes at this time. He even staged, in 1923, a ballet almost as daring as Nijinsky's *Le Sacre du printemps*: *Tanzsymphonia* (*Dance Symphony*) to Beethoven's Fourth Symphony – a one-act ballet with concentrated and boldly imaginative dance-images, which used symbolism rather than a straightforward story. In fact, it aroused much the same mixture of protest and applause as the Nijinsky/Stravinsky ballet.

This violent reaction showed how advanced were Lopukhov's ideas. Indeed, he had been dreaming about staging the ballet as early as 1916, and included in it a good deal of complex symbolism about birth, the growth of life out of destruction, the joy of existence and so on. (Its subtitle was *Greatness of the Universe*, and it ended in a 'cosmogonic spiral'.) Lopukhov used a number of highly talented young dancers, including Georgi Balanchivadze (later to be known as George Balanchine), Leonid Lavrovsky (who went on to create *Romeo and Juliet*) and Alexandra Danilova (who achieved great fame as a ballerina). Unfortunately, the ballet was taken off after only one performance, because some of the movements were considered too daring or even obscene; nevertheless, Lopukhov continued to create controversial ballets up to 1929, as well as his own versions of Diaghilev ballets.

Then the political situation, with Stalin firmly in control, became antipathetic to progress in the arts, and ballet was turned back stylistically almost to the era of Petipa. There could be no question now of anything as artistically advanced as *Tanzsymphonia*. Choreographers now sought a way of continuing to create ballets in the new artistic climate. They found safety by basing their ballets on the works of great writers of the distant past (Pushkin, Lermontov, Gogol, Shakespeare, Balzac, Victor Hugo and Lope de Vega); by keeping their choreography close to classroom steps; and by filling out their ballets so that they lasted an entire evening – as in the days of Petipa.

One of the best of these was Rotislav Zakharov's *The Fountain of Bakhchisaraï* (1934), which he based on a poem by Pushkin. However, the latter, being a great poet, put over his theme in a condensed and poetic way; a faithful realization of it would have resulted in a type of ballet now quite unacceptable, and so the librettist Nikolai

Volkov padded out the poem with a number of additional scenes. In the first act, which includes the heroine Maria's wedding celebrations in the gardens of her father's castle, he brought in her bridegroom Vatslav (a character non-existent in the poem). These celebrations ended with a conventional *pas de deux*, just as they would have done in the days of Petipa. Act II, in which Maria, kidnapped by the Tartar Khan Ghirei, was brought to his capital Bakhchisaraï, was also full of *divertissements*.

Act III was by far the best. Here Zakharov used mime intelligently (in the manner of Fokine) to show the dramatic action clearly: Ghirei's chief wife Zarema, consumed with jealousy, killed Maria with a dagger, and Ghirei ordered his bodyguards to fling Zarema off a high wall down a precipice. In the last act, there was a wild dance of the Tartar warriors, armed with whips. Looking back to the Polovstian Dances choreographed by Ivanov for the opera *Prince Igor*, this had effective ferocity. Indeed, Zakharov could have created a worthy one-act ballet out of his choreography for Acts III and IV, cutting out the padding made necessary by Stalinist policies.

Zakharov, trained in the Stanislavsky Method, did his best to make convincing human beings out of the characters, and created the central role of Maria for Galina Ulanova, who poured feeling and musicality into the *enchaînements* and mime he gave her. Indeed, Ulanova was now emerging as one of the supreme achievements of Soviet

Andris Liepa (son of Maris Liepa) dancing for the Bolshoi Ballet a much-revised variation from Le Corsaire, *a ballet originally choreographed by Mazilier, and re-staged in St Petersburg by Perrot.*

Because of the relatively conventional nature of his choreography and his lavish use of mime, Lavrovsky was able to make the ballet last a complete evening without adding an excessive number of *divertissements*. He also made the fight scenes boldly effective: the artists wielded their swords with admirable spontaneity, as if they actually were Italians of the early Renaissance quite used to wearing (and using) these weapons. The main weakness was the large procession to Juliet's tomb, which went on much too long.

Romeo and Juliet was a great success with the public, both in Leningrad and in Moscow, and when the Bolshoi Ballet took it on tour in the West in 1956, with Ulanova still dancing with supreme artistry, it was a smash hit. Knowing nothing of the work of Lopukhov, spectators accepted it as the supreme achievement of Soviet ballet.

Regrettably, the success of this ballet in the West caused a number of choreographers – and

ballet: a very great dancer, on the same plane as such supreme artists as Pavlova and Karsavina. Ulanova trained in Petrograd, first with her mother and then with the great teacher Agrippina Vaganova (who made a major contribution to the art of ballet by systematizing what she had learned of the Russian 'school' during her years of training with Nicholas Legat) and also some work with Olga Preobrazhenskaya. Ulanova was supreme among the latter's pupils, but other great artists were trained by her in Petrograd/Leningrad, notably Marina Semyonova.

The finest of the multi-act Soviet ballets created in this restrictive artistic climate was given its first performance in Leningrad in 1940 by the Kirov Ballet (given this name in 1935). *Romeo and Juliet* was choreographed by Leonid Lavrovsky to a score by Sergei Prokofiev. Lavrovsky did his best to follow Shakespeare's play as closely as possible, and after many arguments, Prokofiev altered the score (created for an abortive production by the Bolshoi) to fit his demands, composing a number of new pieces and including parts of previous compositions.

Lavrovsky created the choreography in an intelligent and musical manner: prudently, he kept close to classroom steps, but he included a number of soaring lifts for Juliet (supported by Romeo). Ulanova poured such intensity of feeling, musicality and perfection of line into her interpretation that she created a magical effect. She was fortunate in having as her Romeo Konstantin Sergeyev, a fine dancer with an excellent feeling for drama, and Andrei Lopukhov, brother of Fyodor Lopukhov, gave the necessary bite and wit to the role of Mercutio.

TOP LEFT *Galina Ulanova dancing Juliet in Lavrovsky's version of the Prokofiev* Romeo and Juliet, *showing her magical* dusha, *lightness, subtlety and musicality. Her Romeo is Alexander Lapauri. Bolshoi Ballet, c. 1956.*
RIGHT Spartacus, *with choreography by Yuri Grigorovich: a fiery leap by the male* corps de ballet *of the Bolshoi Ballet, 1986.*

directors of ballet companies – there to think that a multi-act ballet was the equivalent of a multi-act opera or play – being inevitably more artistically significant than a one-act ballet. This was despite the fact that Fokine and his many successors had for decades demonstrated very clearly that choreography had become so concentrated in the 20th century that it could tackle any theme, no matter how complex, in an hour or less. Because of the heavy cost of putting on ballets lasting a complete evening, the change of policy to accommodate these dinosaurs cut down the opportunities for creative work in many ballet companies in the West – though fortunately not in all of them.

Within the Soviet Union, on the other hand, *Romeo and Juliet* came as the period of the worthy (even if much padded) multi-act ballets was coming to an end. The Bolshoi Ballet had suffered considerably (like those Western companies that concentrated on full-length ballets) because any such production had to be a success. With so much investment in time and money, no chances could be taken – and the rare new full-length ballets fell far short of *Romeo and Juliet* in quality. However, Yuri Grigorovich, the director of the Bolshoi from 1964, devised one ballet, *Spartacus* (1968), which, despite its melodramatic story and rather obvious choreography, created a sensation because of the fiery and powerful dancing of two splendid male dancers: Vladimir Vasiliev as the noble slave Spartacus, and Maris Liepa as the vicious Roman general Crassus. Choreographically, these two roles were very conventional, but the two great dancers poured such intensity into their characterizations, and danced with such masculine force, that audiences were spellbound. They were also staggered by the impact of a large group of powerful male dancers. Vasiliev danced Spartacus for many years, and so audiences in the West tended to identify him with powerful, very

masculine dancing – whereas he is a sensitive, intelligent and versatile artist, as is Liepa.

As a young dancer, Irek Mukhamedov took over the role of Spartacus and danced it with fire and masculinity, drawing on his own Central Asian background to lay rather more stress on fluidity than Vasiliev.

Up to the early Sixties, the Kirov and the Bolshoi had different attitudes to ballets surviving from the 19th century. The assistant director of the Kirov Theatre, speaking at a press conference in London when the company visited this city for the first time in 1961, described the Kirov's attitude by using an imaginative metaphor: 'We have dozens of Rembrandts in the Hermitage Museum: we do not repaint our Rembrandts.' At this time, however, the choreographers working with the Bolshoi (and, later, the Kirov) kept revising the classics – and revising the revisions – so that the choreography of the ballets was altered almost beyond recognition. Fortunately, *Giselle* remained with only minor changes, as it had been

LEFT *Irek Mukhamedov in the title role of* Spartacus. *Bolshoi Ballet, 1986.*
RIGHT Giselle, *Act II, with Nina Ananiashvili (Giselle) and Andris Liepa (Albrecht) performing Giselle's* leitmotif *dance-image. Bolshoi Ballet, 1986.*

preserved since Perrot restaged it in St Petersburg in 1850; and Fokine's great ballet *Chopiniana* (*Les Sylphides*) was also preserved quite well.

Two outstanding ballerinas – born in the same year, 1925 – emerged within the Bolshoi near the end of the war: Raissa Struchkova and Maya Plisetskaya, who had very different temperaments and styles. Struchkova was adorable in *demi-caractère* roles because of her ebullience; no ballerina could equal her in flashy pieces like *Spring Waters* and *Walpurgisnacht*, which she quite transformed. Plisetskaya's career as a dancer has been much longer. She excelled in dramatic roles: with her fiery personality, her high leaps and her capacity for powerful projection, she imposed her stamp on every character she undertook. In the last act of *Romeo and Juliet*, she projected a love of battle rather than the revolt of a defenceless girl; in the same way she quite transformed *The Dying Swan*, showing it in a heroic battle against death. She chose Tolstoy's novel *Anna Karenina* as the basis for a ballet she choreographed for herself (1972), because it gave her the chance to give a powerful portrayal of rebellious and doomed femininity.

Before the Revolution, the Maryinsky Ballet in St Petersburg was superior to the Bolshoi in Moscow in many ways, and as the Kirov (in Leningrad), it retained its superior quality until the Fifties and early Sixties. But the Soviet government had begun to raise the Bolshoi's standards during the war by bringing to it fine dancers and teachers from the Kirov – above all, Ulanova – and then the Bolshoi took on a series of excellent dancers from the best emerging from Soviet ballet schools. The Kirov also suffered deeply from the defection to the West of three of its best dancers – Rudolf Nureyev, Natalia Makarova and Mikhail Baryshnikov – and the suicide of the superb dancer Yuri Solovyov. Makarova was allowed back in the Soviet Union in 1989 to perform with the Kirov.

A bitter joke was told in the Soviet Union: 'The Kirov is a splendid *corps de ballet* without soloists.' Late in the 1980s, however, fine soloists began to emerge – with exotic names suggesting their origins in Central Asia.

At the Bolshoi, Vasiliev maintains an approach to ballet very different from that of Grigorovich, and goes his own way. In his ballet *Anyuta*, based on a short story by Chekhov, he created for his wife Ekaterina Maximova a delightful role which required her to express a gamut of emotions – joy, sorrow, mischievous flirtatiousness and much else – with himself looking unrecognizable in the mime role of the father. In the skilful construction of his ballet he showed how much he had learned from Lavrovsky; but he evolved a style of his own, suited to the bitter irony and humour of the Chekhov story, and made use of the music commissioned from Valery Gavrilin, with the strong period flavour of its waltzes, polkas and quadrilles.

ABOVE *Curtain call by the Bolshoi Ballet during its British tour, 1986. (L to r) Galina Ulanova, Ludmila Semenyaka, Yuri Grigorovich, Alexander Lavrenyuk, Natalia Bessmertnova, Irek Mukhamedov.*
LEFT *Ekaterina Maximova in the title role of* Anyuta, *re-staged by Vladimir Vasiliev for the Riga Ballet (1987). Finding herself surrounded by admiring young men, Anyuta becomes light-hearted and flirtatious.*

After great dancers retire from the Soviet stage, they continue to work in the studios and theatres, coaching young dancers to prepare them for their debuts in major roles such as Giselle. Ulanova has been an imaginative and sensitive coach ever since she took in hand her first protégée, Maximova; and, since then, she has taken the greatest pains with a number of other promising young dancers. She does not impose her own interpretation on a dancer: like every outstanding coach, she helps the dancer to perfect her own interpretation – and each of her protégées dances Giselle in a different way. Raissa Struchkova has shown remarkable flair for coaching in her work with Nina Ananiashvili, constantly correcting and improving every detail of her performances in each role she tackles. This is one of several aspects of ballet in which Western companies learn from the Soviets. The Azerbaijan Ballet, in *Prometheus*, has shown how an ancient myth can be imaginatively interpreted, with skilful use of national traditions of dance and music. In fact, this myth possibly originated in Azerbaijan's oilfield flames.

CHAPTER FIFTEEN

French and Franco-Belgian Ballet

French ballet had been sadly decadent for a long time when the Russians arrived in Paris in 1909. The Paris Opéra Ballet was riddled with intrigue, the standard of teaching was low, the French 'school' was in tatters, and the leading female roles were given to imported Italian stars. In fact, the Opéra Ballet was so resistant to change that, for a long time, the visits of the Diaghilev ballet made hardly any impact on the company. What did give distinction to the performances of the Opéra Ballet for some years was the dancing in roles such as Giselle of the great Russian ballerina Olga Spessivtseva, *étoile* of the company from 1925 to 1932.

In 1929, after the death of Diaghilev and the dissolution of his company, Serge Lifar joined the Opéra Ballet as director, choreographer and *étoile*. In addition, a number of great Russian dancers who had emigrated from the Soviet Union after the Revolution began to teach in Paris. The work of Olga Preobrazhenskaya was of special importance. She had been forced by a weak back to study in detail the workings of the body in the execution of ballet steps, and – with Nicholas Legat – she used this knowledge to play a primary role in the formation of the Russian 'school'. In Paris, her classes attracted children of Russian *emigrés*, and she did wonders with them.

One highly talented French dancer began training at the Paris Opéra School and then went on to train with Russian teachers – notably Boris Kniaseff and Viktor Gsovsky. In this way, Yvette Chauviré mastered the Russian 'school', and became the first great French ballerina to emerge since Léontine Beaugrand. As Giselle, she was superb – performing the role with the delicate grace of the old French 'school' (as do the Russians) and adding her own very French quality. Lifar gave her a series of leading roles in his ballets, but these gave her only limited opportunities to show the full variety of her talent – as the

Roland Petit's Carmen, *with Zizi Jeanmaire as Carmen and Petit as Don José in the flamboyantly erotic bedroom scene. Les Ballets de Paris, c. 1950.*

finest French dancer of her day. As a guest artist with other companies, she showed a remarkable range – being, for example, outstanding as the Ballerina in *Petrushka*, dancing with Massine.

Roland Petit, who trained at the Opéra, emerged towards the end of the Second World War as a fine dancer and promising choreographer. In 1945, he formed his first company, Les Ballets des Champs-Elysées, which, in Paris and on tour, performed ballets by Petit that were lights charming and sexy – a complete break with Lifar's more pretentious style. Three years later, he left this company to form the Ballets de Paris, for which he staged, among others, *Les Demoiselles de la nuit*. Depicting cats on a sloping roof, this had wit, humour and elegance, and it allowed Margot Fonteyn – as Agathe, the white cat – to show her remarkable flair for *demi-caractère* roles, a flair which was neglected in the Sadler's Wells Royal Ballet.

Petit's most successful ballet, *Carmen* (1949), owed much to the elegant legs and extraordinary talent of Zizi Jeanmaire. Trained in the Russian 'school' by Kniaseff after her start at the Paris Opéra School, she was gifted with an astonishing flair for playing characters that were sexy, sophisticated, charming and impudent; in fact, she was an ideal *demi-caractère* dancer. Much of *Carmen* was naive, but it had a witty set and costumes by Antoni Clavé, and in the erotic bedroom scene, Zizi was irresistibly teasing and seductive.

BELOW LEFT *Violette Verdy (touchingly brave and tender as the Bride) and Roland Petit (as the Wolf) making the most of Petit's choreography. Les Ballets de Paris, c. 1953.*
RIGHT *Maurice Béjart's* Songs of a Wayfarer, *with Eric Vu-An and Peter Schaufuss (kneeling), guest-artist of the London Festival Ballet.*
OVERLEAF *Eric Vu-An taking a splendid leap in the leading role of Béjart's* The Kabuki, 47 Samurai, *created for the Tokyo Ballet.*

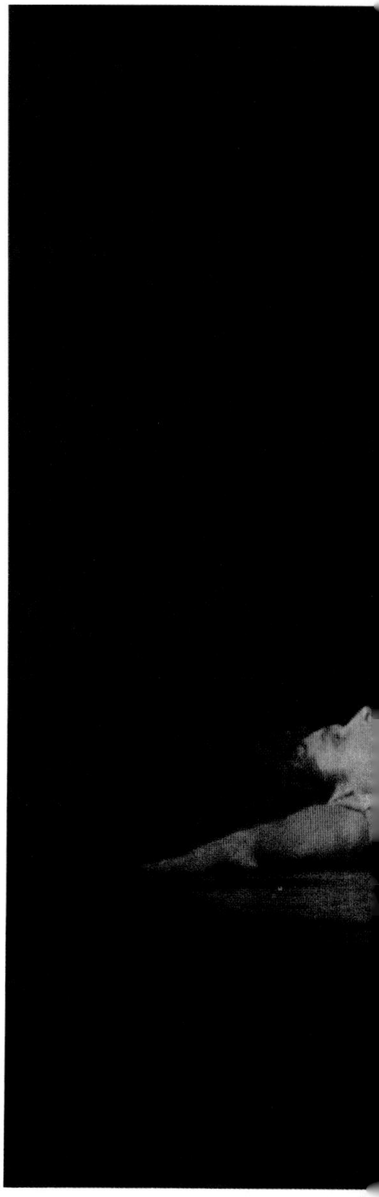

The last of the young Petit's successful ballets was *Le Loup* (1953), in which he portrayed a wolf. The heroine – delightfully interpreted by Violette Verdy – is tricked into believing that her faithless fiancé has been turned into a wolf, and she falls in love with the beast and follows it into the forest, where both are hunted to death. This ballet could easily have become embarrassingly sentimental, but Petit and Verdy danced with such animation and assurance that it came off.

Another French choreographer, emerging soon after Petit, was totally different in style and temperament. This was Maurice Béjart, an artist with a flair for expressionism and striking visual effects. In fact, he is a superb showman, with a very strong personality and an amazing gift for renewing himself, so that he has been able to create one striking spectacle after another, for decade after decade.

His career took off when he formed his Ballet of the 20th Century in Brussels, associated with the great opera house, the Théâtre Royal de la Monnaie. The company he formed was an international one, with dancers from many countries, and he and they toured very widely. In Brussels, he gave some performances at the Monnaie, but for his big spectacles, he liked to show the ballet in a big circular hall, with audiences sitting around the dancers – leaving only about one-fifth of the circle for the set – and entrances and exits were often made through the audience. In a typical piece, *Nijinsky, Clown de Dieu* (*Nijinsky, Clown of God*: 1971), he gave his own version of fragments of ballets in which Nijinsky appeared, as if remembered by the dancer after he went mad. Diaghilev, feared and hated by Nijinsky, was shown as a giant puppet with a dancer inside – and a long arm resting on an attendant, so that he could maintain his balance.

The company had equal numbers of male and female dancers, but Béjart showed himself mainly concerned with choreographing for the men – above all, Jorge Donn and Paolo Bortoluzzi. However, in *Roméo et Juliette* (1966), he created an extraordinary solo for Maina Gielgud – who, as Queen Mab, danced the equivalent of the speech describing Queen Mab that, in Shakespeare's play, is spoken by Mercutio.

Béjart has a great interest in Indian dancing, and created for Gielgud a somewhat oriental dance using authentic Indian music in his ballet *Bakhti*. When he founded a school in Brussels to train artists so that they could take part in 'total theatre' productions, he called the school 'Mudra' – the Sanskrit word for a symbolic gesture.

Béjart is an expressionist in his own way. When, early in his career, he used Ravel's *Boléro* – in

which one simple rhythm builds steadily to a climax – he had a female dancer performing one simple step in the middle of a round table, surrounded by a large group of men who seemed hypnotized by her. Later, he gave the central role to Jorge Donn, and finally he had the whole ballet performed by men. The choreography could hardly be simpler, but in its bold and brash way, it is striking. Béjart has kept this expressionist ballet in his repertoire since 1960 – a year after he began work in Brussels – and he has shown a similar affection for an even earlier expressionist ballet, his version of *The Rite of Spring* (1959). When, in later years, he explored fields such as oriental mysticism and Kabuki, he retained his penchant for expressionism.

Always a go-getter, Béjart organized the first joint performance of a Western and a Soviet company when in 1987 he and Oleg Vinogradov (director of the Kirov Ballet) brought together the Kirov and Béjart's Ballet of the 20th Century in *White Nights*, a televized dance spectacular in which dancers of both companies performed on stages set up on islands in the Neva river, among huge columns in front of Kazan Cathedral, in parks, in a theatre and so on, during the 'white nights' of Leningrad in midsummer when it never gets quite dark. Extracts from *Chopiniana*, *Les Sylphides* and the Kingdom of the Shades from *La Bayadère*, performed by the Kirov Ballet, looked wrong in the open air without stage lighting; but the Béjart ballets suffered less, and the male Kirov dancers did well in Béjart's choreography.

The most effective extract came from *Seven Greek Dances*: here Béjart had two of his best male dancers perform skilfully balletized *demi-caractère* versions of Greek traditional dances.

A month later, in July, Béjart took his company to Lausanne, and made his headquarters at the Palais de Beaulieu in this Swiss city. He now called his company Béjart Ballet Lausanne.

During the Eighties, the Paris Opéra made an extraordinary leap forward. Under the leadership of Rudolf Nureyev, it established itself once again as one of the finest companies in the world, at a time when many big ones were declining artistically. For years, attempts had been made to induce Nureyev to come to Paris, but he had always refused – knowing that intrigues within the Opéra would cripple his authority. Finally, in 1983, he secured agreement to a contract which gave him real authority as artistic director.

Under his direction, the company flowered. An extraordinary group of outstanding young artists came to the fore, superbly trained and able to take over major roles with individuality, grace, charm and a glorious sense of style. Although their dancing was based on the Russian 'school', it had its own, very French qualities: a new French 'school' was emerging. The company was now very large – comprising dancers associated with both the Paris Opéra and the Opéra Comique – and Nureyev was able to take good advantage of the fact that he had two theatres at his disposal, as well as the opportunity to use other theatres.

One of his most extraordinary achievements was to introduce Tudor's ballets to France. Although Tudor had been deeply influenced by French culture, and his dramatic ballets were strongly influenced by Proust, his work had remained unknown in France. Fortunately, Tudor and Nureyev were great friends, with great respect for each other, and they jointly arranged for the presentation of an all-Tudor programme at the Salle Favart (previously known as the Opéra Comique). This made a tremendous impact, first on the dancers who had rehearsed the ballets (which presented them with many new challenges) and then on spectators. They all discovered, to their astonishment, the existence of a great choreographer who, in some ways, was intensely French – notably in his care for nuances of feeling

Nureyev's version of the Prokofiev Romeo and Juliet, *staged by him for the Paris Opéra Ballet in 1984, with Monique Loudières as Juliet and Patrick Dupont as Romeo.*

LEFT *The first* 'Hommage à Antony Tudor' *season presented by Nureyev with the Paris Opéra Ballet in 1985. As Caroline, in* Jardin aux lilas, *Yannick Stéphant shows poetic vulnerability and despair.* BELOW LEFT Equinoxe, *with choreography by Gigi Caciuleanu, performed by the Théâtre Chorégraphique de Rennes. Caciuleanu in a comic leap.*

and his capacity for achieving a combination of restraint and deep emotion.

Helped by the advice of Tudor's first great dancer, Maude Lloyd, Nureyev succeeded magnificently with his *Hommage à Antony Tudor* – so much so that it became an annual institution. Danced by the French artists, the very complex Tudor ballets sprang to life. Since *Jardin aux lilas* is very French in a Proustian way, the success of the French dancers in that particular ballet was not surprising, but they did equally well in the very austere and very Nordic choreography of *Dark Elegies*, understanding the need for sincerity and understatement. The programme was a triumph for Nureyev, who showed remarkable insight in his casting, using both promising young soloists such as Karin Averty and established artists such

as Isabelle Guérin. In later years, *étoiles* – impressed by the ballets – persuaded Nureyev to let them take over the leading roles, and interpreted them superbly. It was clear that the Tudor ballets had found a home that would preserve their rare qualities.

Another of Nureyev's extraordinary achievements in Paris was to foster the development of a remarkable group of principal dancers – promoting them at an early age if they showed outstanding talent. This happened to Sylvie Guillem, who took her place as an *étoile* with unchallengeable authority alongside other artists of exceptional quality, such as the aforementioned Isabelle Guérin, Monique Loudières and Eric Vu-An.

Guillem joined the Royal Ballet as guest artist for three years in 1989.

The French government now has a policy calling for the decentralization of ballet, with companies established in provincial cities, all with national status. One such, the Théâtre Chorégraphique de Rennes, was established by the Rumanian-born Gigi Caciuleanu – a choreographer who has shown extraordinary talent ever since 1968 when, as a young dancer, he presented a delightful solo (self-choreographed) at the international ballet competition at Varna in Bulgaria. What he showed then was so witty and delightful that it won a well-deserved award; and in the ballets he creates for the company in Rennes, he maintains an astonishing level of wit, charm, originality and poetry. The Rennes repertoire – stressing humour, but also including serious works – is unlike that of any other company. To achieve the type of movements he wants from his artists, Caciuleanu has developed his own technique of modern dance, and gives the daily company class himself.

CHAPTER SIXTEEN

Denmark and Sweden

Denmark

It was fortunate, but not too surprising, that the art of ballet was able to remain alive in Russia in the second half of the 19th century. The Imperial Russian Ballet was subsidized out of the colossal revenues of the autocratic tsars, and so was able to preserve a large number of venerable ballets right up to the 20th century, irrespective of their popularity with the public. In the same way, teaching traditions were preserved for decade after decade: thus Christian Johansson could pass on the techniques of the old French 'school' (then in decay in France) to great dancers such as Nicholas Legat and Olga Preobrazhenskaya, who became pioneer teachers of the new Russian 'school'.

Denmark, however, is a tiny country compared with Russia, and the survival of ballet there as a major art of the theatre was a near-miracle. It was thanks to the immense prestige of August Bournonville that it was maintained at a good level during decades of decadence, and a considerable number of Bournonville ballets were preserved. Thanks to him, Danish ballet was, and is, a source of national pride. Every year young boys and girls are sent by their parents to audition for the Royal Danish Ballet School – for ballet dancing has never been regarded by Danish parents as a career unfit for men, as it was (and still is, to some extent) elsewhere in Europe, apart from the Soviet Union.

In the Thirties, Forties, and Fifties, three Danish artists did wonders in maintaining high standards in the classics and the Fokine and Bournonville ballets: the two great dancers Margot Lander and Børge Ralov, and the director of the Royal Danish Ballet, Harald Lander. Unlike his predecessors, Lander had studied abroad – mastering the Russian 'school' through his work in the United States and the Soviet Union. Just before he left Denmark in 1952, he arranged for the great Russian teacher Vera Volkova to be brought to Copenhagen, where she taught the Russian 'school' – as codified by Vaganova – to the Royal Danish dancers for the rest of her life, contributing much to Danish ballet.

August Bournonville's A Legend *with Peter Martins of the Royal Danish Ballet dancing 'the flying Danish embrace', the powerful but elegant jump typical of the Danish male style.*

Harald Lander's lasting achievement as a choreographer was *Etudes* (1948), which was totally cosmopolitan in style. Essentially it was a showpiece for dancers, beginning with a stylized presentation of the *barre*-work of a ballet class, and then showing the dancers moving through *enchaînements* of greater and greater difficulty, until they reached a dazzling finale. The ballet was a great success in Denmark, and came to be performed by many companies.

Flemming Flindt, director of the Royal Danish Ballet from 1966 to 1978 (during which time Bournonville ballets were neglected), did well with one of his own ballets, *The Lesson* (1963), based on a one-act play by Ionesco about a girl who comes for a grammar lesson (transformed in the ballet into a dance lesson) at the studio of a sinister teacher. Flindt's choreography was far from inspired, but the interaction between the teacher and the pupil, derived from Ionesco and shown mainly in mime, offered splendid opportunities for gifted artists. (In mime, a dancer has a greater chance of achieving fine things with mediocre choreography than in dancing.) The Danish dancer Niels Kehlet was fascinating as the murderous teacher – as also was Nureyev in the role. Mette Hønningen did very well as the girl.

Peter Schaufuss, the son of two outstanding Danish dancers (Frank Schaufuss and Mona Vangsaae), was fortunate in being, like his contemporary Eva Evdokimova, one of the last people to be trained in the Bournonville 'school' before the Bournonville classes were dropped for some years. Schaufuss developed into a dancer of fine quality, and after performing for a time with the company he began to guest with other companies outside Denmark, including London Festival Ballet, leading to his staging a fine production of Bournonville's *La Sylphide* for this company, and then becoming its artistic director.

The supreme achievement of Henning Kronstam, artistic director from 1979 to 1985, was to stage a Bournonville Festival in 1979, marking the 100th anniversary of Bournonville's death. Spectators and critics came from all over the world to see the splendid Bournonville heritage which had survived in Denmark and was now being revived. From then on, Bournonville's place in the Royal Danish Ballet repertoire was assured, and this much-prized heritage is now studied in detail in Copenhagen.

RIGHT *Flemming Flindt's* The Lesson, *with Flindt as the teacher and Anne Marie Vessel as the pupil. Royal Danish Ballet.*

BELOW Etudes, *created by Harald Lander in 1948 in cosmopolitan style, as a showpiece for the Royal Danish Ballet. It shows how well the Danish dancers can cope with severe challenges.*

Sweden

Ballet has a long history in Sweden, having been established on a professional basis in 1773 by King Gustav III, as part of an opera company. The twenty-four dancers were mainly French, as was the ballet master Gallodier. King Gustav III loved the theatre, wrote dramas and operas, appeared on stage, and built his own court theatre at Drottningholm, near the royal palace just outside Stockholm – a theatre which survives to this day with its stage machinery and many of the settings and costumes from King Gustav's time. Noverre was so impressed by this company (expanded to include seventy-two dancers) that he prepared an elaborate prospectus, which he sent to the king, in the hope of securing an engagement. The king showed poor judgement in turning down Noverre, but the latter's influence became strong when his pupil, Antoine Bournonville (father of August) became ballet master in 1781.

Although the great dancer Charles Didelot was born in Stockholm, and was sent by the Swedish king to Paris to study, he chose to make his career in London, St Petersburg and other big cities. The half-Swedish Marie Taglioni also left, to become a cosmopolitan superstar, and the leading Swedish dancer, Christian Johansson, became a teacher in St Petersburg.

Ballet decayed in Sweden in the second half of the 19th century as it did elsewhere. Then Fokine came to the Royal Swedish Ballet in 1913 and trained some fine dancers, who became the leading artists in Les Ballets Suédois, founded in Paris by Rolf de Maré, patron of the arts and collector, in 1920. De Maré commissioned the Fokine-trained dancer Jean Börlin to stage a number of ballets using some of the most imaginative artists and composers working in Paris, and offering real competition to Diaghilev through the quality of the themes, sets, costumes and music, even though the Swedish dancers were less expressive than Diaghilev's. The most striking of the ballets presented by de Maré were expressionist/surrealist in style and theme, more akin to developments in contemporary German modern dance than to the ballets staged by Diaghilev.

In *L'Homme et son désir* (*Man and His Desire*, 1921), the central figure was a quasi-abstract symbol: Man, robbed of personality by night and sleep, and dreaming strange dreams (which were represented by figures in faceless masks). The designer André Parr provided Börlin with a series of levels on which the dancers could move, and the three chief characters (The Man, The Woman and The Other Woman) danced in bare feet, like modern German expressionist dancers. The composer was Darius Milhaud, and the nature of the ballet was largely determined by the ideas of the writer Paul Claudel, who wrote the libretto.

Like the Ballets Russes of Diaghilev, the Ballets Suédois existed outside the home country of the company members, and so had little impact in Sweden – indeed, at this time, the Royal Swedish Ballet was in the doldrums. However, it began to move ahead in 1949 when Joel Berglund, the newly appointed *Intendant* of the Royal Theatre in Stockholm, invited Tudor to come and work with the company – knowing that Tudor was free to come, since Ballet Theatre had been closed down for some time.

On his arrival, Tudor found that he would have a difficult time achieving a satisfactory standard in Stockholm, since the dancers were technically weak. However, he set to work with great *élan* and energy, training the dancers and staging three ballets which he felt would give them the right sort of challenge: *Jardin aux lilas*, *Gala Performance* and *Giselle*. Fortunately, he was able to use a very talented half-Russian ballerina, Ellen Rasch, and he set the company on an upward path. After he returned to the United States in 1953, the British teacher and producer Mary Skeaping took over, and worked hard to raise the standard of dancing.

When Tudor returned in 1961, he found a more impressive company, with a number of fine Swedish dancers. Now he was able to stage ballets as challenging as *Pillar of Fire*, *Romeo and Juliet* and *Dark Elegies*, taking advantage of the talents of such artists as Mariane Orlando, Gerd Andersson and Berit Skøld. Swedish audiences much appreciated his work, and he liked working in Sweden so much that he even consented to create a new ballet, *Echoing of Trumpets* (1963).

L'Homme et son désir, *dream-like ballet choreographed by Jean Börlin for Les Ballets Suédois in 1921. Börlin (in front of diamond shape) dances the leading role of the Man.*

Tudor had a habit of distancing himself from his themes by setting his ballets in the past, or in no specific period, but Swedish audiences wanted a new Tudor ballet that was very obviously contemporary. To that end, he created one about the horrors of war in the present day – for once, dealing with the action in a straightforward manner, but doing this with great skill. The Swedish *danseuses* did wonders with both *Pillar of Fire* and *Dark Elegies*, and were strongly dramatic in *Echoing of Trumpets*; however, some of the male dancers were less impressive.

The Swedish choreographer Birgit Cullberg trained for four years with Jooss and Leeder in England (1935–39), and began to create ballets in Sweden in 1946, drawing on her experience with the two German artists. Her finest ballet, *Miss Julie*, was based on the powerful play by August Strindberg about an aristocratic girl who finds herself out of her depth when she indulges in an affair with a valet. Cullberg's choreography was

LEFT *Birgit Åkesson in* Minor Seconds, Major Sevenths, *danced to music from Bartók's* Microcosmos. *The mysterious, dream-like dance-images of her solo convey impressions beyond the reach of words.*
TOP RIGHT Adam and Eve, *with choreography by Birgit Cullberg, performed by the Cullberg Ballet. Mona Elgh as Eve and Niklas Ek as Adam.*

competent, and the story was so strong that the two fine Swedish artists who took the leading roles – Elsa-Marianne von Rosen and Julius Mengarelli – were able to make the ballet intensely dramatic.

Birgit Åkesson was a supremely gifted and original Swedish modern dancer who trained with Wigman and joined the Wigman company in 1931. She came to feel stifled as a member of the chorus, so she left and went to Paris where she mixed with leading painters and composers, and formed a style and technique all her own, quite remote from expressionism. In *Eye: Sleep in Dream*, for example, she began by using her hands to suggest light shining down into water; she became the light – and then she became the fish swimming through the water. As the dance progressed, she moved in a poetic and dream-like way through some very strange positions, sometimes keeping her body close to the ground in deep *pliés*; indeed, she used a technique more akin to Balinese dancing than to any Western modern-dance technique. She became much respected in Sweden, where her extraordinary originality was appreciated, and when she danced in the United States in 1957, she made a strong impression on both Tudor and Martha Graham. Some of her finest dances have been preserved on film and tape.

Stockholm is fortunate in having the Dansmuseet, the only museum in the world that is devoted solely to dance. This was established in 1951 by Bengt Hägar, with the help of funds from Rolf de Maré, and is now a thriving institution, with an immense collection drawn from all over the world, covering every form of dance.

CHAPTER SEVENTEEN

Germany

Stuttgart was a great creative centre of ballet in the 18th century, when the Duke of Württemberg provided Noverre with the funds needed to enlarge the local company by engaging a number of the finest French dancers of the day. After Noverre left for Vienna, the company continued, but on a much reduced scale, and lost its leading position in the ballet world.

During the 1920s, German modern dance came to Stuttgart, as it did to other German cities. Indeed, Oskar Schlemmer staged his *Triadic Ballet* – with the dancers dressed in weird costumes – in Stuttgart in 1922, before moving to the Bauhaus design centre in Weimar.

After Hitler came to power, most modern dancers were able to continue working all over Germany – unless, of course, they were Jewish. When a *Gauleiter* was appointed with the power to regulate dance, their activities were more constricted, but usually they did not feel it necessary to leave Germany.

John Cranko's version of the Stravinsky ballet Jeu de Cartes, *performed by the Stuttgart Ballet in 1969. The Joker (Egon Madsen) crawls under the other cards.*

After the war, German attitudes to dance changed decisively. Whereas, before, the *Intendants* of opera houses had used ballet dancers mainly to provide dances in operas, and creativity was concentrated on modern dance, now the public had an overwhelming desire to see ballet. In a Germany where most of the cities were reduced to rubble, and the future seemed very uncertain, people felt a desperate need for classical dancing, with no hint of expressionism. Ballet seemed to offer order, security, a link with the Germany of the 19th century – long before Hitler, long before the two wars which had turned out so disastrously.

However, it was difficult for the opera houses to stage ballets of quality: there were few talented ballet dancers in the country, and no tradition of balletic choreography which could be revived. Some modern dancers attempted to create ballets in the opera houses and municipal theatres, but they lacked the knowledge and experience needed for this. Even Kurt Jooss, when he arrived in Essen in 1951, failed to re-establish his fusion of modern dance and ballet.

It was a turning point, not just for the Stuttgart Ballet but for German ballet as a whole, when Walter Erich Schäfer, *Intendant* of the Württembergisches Staatstheater in Stuttgart, invited John Cranko to take over the ballet company in 1961.

Cranko, a South African, had trained at the University of Cape Town Ballet School, but as soon as there was civilian transportation (which had disappeared during the war) to take him there, he came to London (1946). He continued his training at the Sadler's Wells School, and then joined the Sadler's Wells Ballet as a dancer. But his real interest was choreography; indeed, he had created his first ballets for the University of Cape Town Theatre Ballet while he was still in his teens. Of all the ballets he staged in London, *Pineapple Poll* (1951) stood out because of its gentle humour and absence of padding.

He worked under ideal conditions in Stuttgart. Supported by Schäfer, he was able to bring in fine young dancers from a good many countries, and to mould them as he wished. His standard of choreography improved, and his leading dancers proved to be remarkable artists. Above all, there was Marcia Haydée, who came to the company in 1961 after training with Russian teachers in Río de Janeiro, at the Sadler's Wells School, and with the leading Russian teachers Preobrazhenskaya and Egorova in Paris, as well as dancing with the

LEFT *Cranko's version for the Stuttgart Ballet of the Prokofiev* Romeo and Juliet, *as performed in 1969, with Richard Cragun (at right) superbly intense as Romeo, fighting Tybalt.* BELOW *Marcia Haydée as Tatiana in Cranko's* Onegin*: the last act, after Tatiana has married and has tried to forget Onegin. Haydée is partnered by Jan Stripling. Stuttgart Ballet, 1969.*

company of the Marquis de Cuevas. She developed into a remarkable dramatic dancer, and Cranko gave her the leading female roles in most of his ballets. Another outstanding artist – like Haydée, a splendid dramatic dancer – was the American artist Richard Cragun, who joined the company in 1962, and was soon taking leading roles.

Rapidly Cranko built up the company, creating new ballets himself (showing a preference for multi-act ballets), as well as staging new versions of Diaghilev ballets and of the Prokofiev *Romeo and Juliet*, and inviting other choreographers to create ballets for the company. The support he received from Schäfer and the public was invaluable: Cranko was able to increase the number of performances, so that instead of an occasional evening of ballet, the company performed several times a week; and the theatre was well equipped with rehearsal rooms. He brought in Anne Woolliams, an English dancer and teacher, trained in London by Espinosa and Volkova, as teacher of the Stuttgart company and school.

It was not long before people began talking of this company as *das deutsche Ballettwunder* – 'the German ballet miracle' – for it had reached an international standard, and was able to go on extensive foreign tours. Cranko's version of *Romeo and Juliet* was skilful and impressive, though it lacked the musicality of the Lavrovsky

Thom Schilling's production of Swan Lake *for the Komische Oper Ballet, East Berlin, with Jutta Deutschland as Odette and Dieter Hulse as Prince Siegfried.*

version. His masterpiece was *Onegin* (1965), based on the famous novel-poem by Pushkin and using music by Tchaikovsky (while avoiding the music of the latter's opera *Eugene Onegin*). Here was a ballet almost without padding, and with a skilful blending of mime and dancing. As in the Lavrovsky ballet, Cranko used *enchaînements* which, though keeping quite close to the classroom, were put together with such skill and taste that they allow the dancers to pour feeling into them.

At first, Haydée, as Tatiana, suggests a girl who is young, romantic, impulsive, shy and innocent. She then shows a remarkable transformation to an elegant and mature married woman living in high society in the city – a woman who is still in love with Onegin, but feels she must reject him. The title role, created by Ray Barra, was later taken over by Richard Cragun – who danced and acted it so superbly that he established himself as one of the finest dramatic dancers in the world. He is magnificent as he projects Onegin's cool arrogance, above all when he tears up Tatiana's letter, treating it as evidence of a young girl's passing infatuation; then, quite transformed on meeting the mature Tatiana, he shows a desperate love for her, bitterly regretting that he has wronged her.

Cranko did much to encourage young choreographers, and his influence on German ballet was enormous; it was still growing at the time of his death in 1973, while returning by plane from an American tour with his company. Glen Tetley (with his fusion of modern dance and ballet) was then made *Ballettdirektor*, but he was not a success, and Haydée took over the post, showing firm authority as she carried on the Cranko tradition.

In many ways, the Stuttgart Ballet is typical of German ballet companies, with dancers from many countries – drawn from the hundreds who audition each year. But the ballet company of the Komische Oper in East Berlin is very different. Here Tom Schilling – able to draw on his early training in German modern dance as well as on ballet traditions, and having profited greatly from his years working under the great opera producer Felsenstein – has been able to build up a fine company of German dancers, and create imaginative ballets, with an admirable variety of themes.

Among the finest – and most complex – of his ballets is *Elective Affinities*, based on Goethe's novel. In this, he shows the changing relationships between four characters, and brings the ballet to a fine climax with the beautiful and very sad death scene of Ottilie, who is in such distress that she lets herself die of hunger. Here the versatile Schilling shows himself well-attuned to the early flowering of romanticism in German literature – previously the inspiration of both *Giselle* and *Coppélia*.

CHAPTER EIGHTEEN

Alicia Alonso and Cuban Ballet

The astonishing rise of the National Ballet of Cuba, in the second half of this century, is above all due to the wide experience, artistry, imagination, intelligence, good judgement, independence of mind, gift for leadership and almost incredible capacity for hard work of Alicia Alonso. It is mainly thanks to her devotion and patience – and the example she has set by her superb dancing – that such a magnificent company, one of the world's finest, has come into existence on a small and undeveloped island.

The artistic policy she has developed in Cuba is so fruitful, and embraces such diversity, that she takes her place as one of the very few truly creative artistic directors, in a line which stretches back through Marie Rambert and Diaghilev to Count Durazzo. Unlike the others, however, she has also had a magnificent career as a prima ballerina, and has continued to dance for a longer period than any other in history. It is amazing to consider that she was able to celebrate fifty years of dancing on stage – while still continuing to dance leading roles.

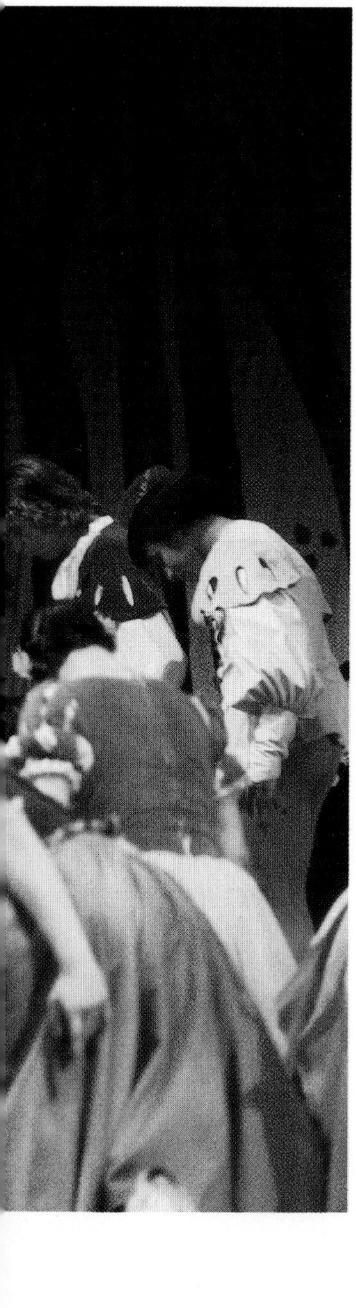

LEFT *Shakespeare's* Hamlet, *imaginatively condensed and stylized by Iván Tenorio, with Mariá Elena Llorente as Ophelia. National Ballet of Cuba, 1984.*
ABOVE RIGHT *Crucial to Alicia Alonso's artistic development has been her interpretation of the role of Giselle, here danced with the great* danseur noble *Igor Youskevitch. Ballet Theatre, 1953.*

When very young, she began her training in ballet in Havana, and then went to New York, where she continued with a number of distinguished Russian teachers. She was very fortunate to arrive there when she did, for she was able to join Ballet Theatre in 1940, soon after its formation. This gave her the opportunity to work with distinguished choreographers – especially Antony Tudor, who gave her leading roles in his ballets. From his teaching, she and her husband, Fernando Alonso, became familiar with what one might call the Tudor–English 'school', with its combination of elements from the Cecchetti Method and the Russian 'school', and Tudor's own highly developed musicality. When he created *Undertow* in 1945, he gave her the important role of Ate, which made great demands on her dramatic ability; and in 1948, in *Shadow of the Wind* (based on Mahler's symphony *Das Lied von der Erde/Song of the Earth*), he gave her another very exacting part to dance, that of the abandoned wife. When Balanchine created *Theme and Variations* for Ballet Theatre in 1947, he gave Alonso the leading role, taking good advantage of both her musicality and her astonishing technical

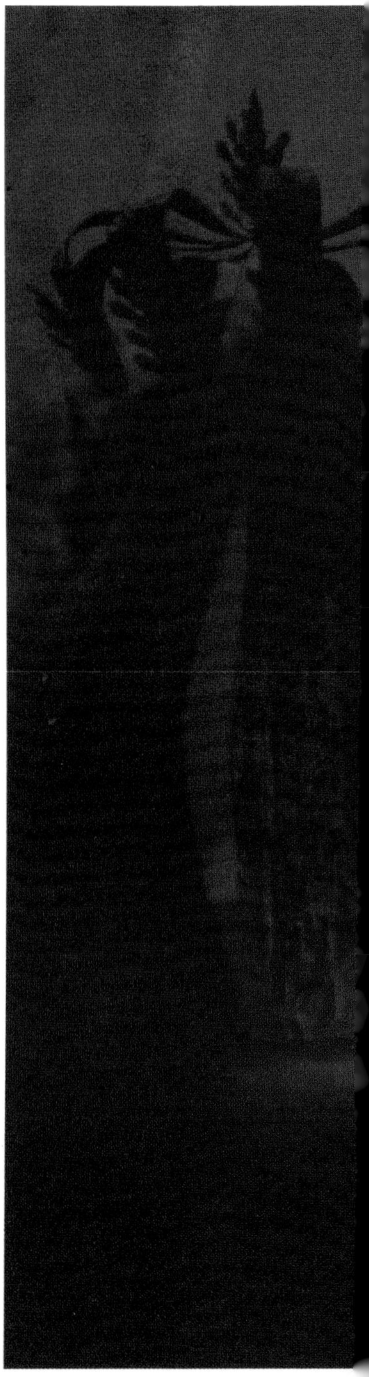

ABOVE Hamlet, *with Lázaro Carreño in the title role and Maria Elena Llorente as Ophelia. National Ballet of Cuba, 1984.*
RIGHT *Cuban National Ballet's.* Electra Garrigó *with Ofelia Gonzalez and the corps de ballet.*

prowess: she executed the most difficult feats with such ease that she quite disguised the immense skill involved. Such was her versatility that she showed equal polish and spontaneity in ballets by Fokine and the 19th-century classics as well as modern ballets. Romanticism, malicious humour, ferocity, and the carefully hidden sadness of a Chinese wife: all these styles and moods seemed to come naturally to her, though of course she worked very hard at them, and profited a great deal from the advice given her by choreographers and producers.

Notwithstanding her great success in America, as well as on tour outside the United States with Ballet Theatre, she never forgot that she was a Cuban – and a very patriotic one, with a deep love of her country. She longed to establish a ballet company there, and succeeded in doing so in 1948, and also founded a school, which would provide dancers for the company. However, she came up against severe obstacles: under the Battista regime, it was extremely difficult for her to obtain finance for the company; and Cuban parents were loth to send their children to a ballet school which did not seem to offer good chances of employment. It was particularly hard to induce parents to send their boys for training in ballet since – as in most countries – ballet was considered too effeminate an art to be a satisfactory career for men.

Even so, she and her husband were able to proceed with the formation of a 'school' appropriate to Cubans – exuberant people living in a tropical climate – and took only those elements from the Russian, Tudor–English and Italian 'schools' that were suitable. This work went ahead at a great rate after the Cuban revolution, when the company was established as the National Ballet of Cuba, with ample funds at its disposal, and a school with studios admirably adapted to the Cuban climate. It was not long before Cuban dancers were showing their great quality by winning prizes at international competitions, where they had to compete with the finest young dancers from all over the world.

Ethnically, Cuba is very mixed. Descendants of slaves from Africa have intermarried with people whose ancestors came from Spain and other European countries, and every possible colour of skin is to be seen. The National Ballet of Cuba

paid no attention to skin colour, and dancers were no longer dependent on money from their parents to start training. At first, it was still difficult to obtain boys for the school: Alicia Alonso solved this problem by going to an orphanage and offering the boys a chance to leave and train for an exciting career.

The repertoire expanded rapidly, initially with a strong emphasis on the standard ballets of the international repertoire: *Giselle*, *Swan Lake*, *Coppélia*, *Les Sylphides*, the Polovtsian Dances from *Prince Igor*, *Petrushka*, *L'Après-midi d'un faune*, Balanchine's *Apollo*, *Le Spectre de la rose*, Nijinska's version of *La Fille mal gardée*, *The Nutcracker*. Alicia Alonso's production of *Giselle* (1952) was of great importance, for she had studied everything she could about this ballet, and worked out the details of her own staging with extreme care. What is more, Giselle was one of her favourite roles, with a kind of romanticism which appealed deeply to her; and she danced superbly in her own production.

One of Alicia Alonso's most astonishing achievements was to foster the development of a group of talented choreographers, who kept abreast of the state of the art while developing their own individual approaches to choreography. Unlike Durazzo and Diaghilev (who both favoured one choreographer at a time), Alonso eventually succeeded in keeping five or more talented choreographers in action simultaneously, and, what is more, she gave them the chance of creating a number of ballets each year. This meant that they had the freedom to try out new ideas, for it did not matter if any one ballet was a success or not. In addition, they had the chance of showing their ballets at the international festivals which take place in Cuba every two or three years – and so could register their impact on an international audience, including a good many critics from other countries. Under such circumstances, they had every inducement to produce ballets which – no matter how Cuban their themes – were of international quality, just as the ballets taken to the West from Russia by Diaghilev had been in the golden age of his company. The standard of Cuban choreography rose year after year because of the encouraging atmosphere in which the ballets were staged: in this respect, they were like those created in the Thirties at the Ballet Club in London.

The choreographers differ so much in style and approach that it is hard to credit that almost all of them are Cuban. Alberto Mendez is distinguished by the subtlety of moods in his best work – notably in *Tarde en la siesta*, the rare quality of which has gained it a permanent place in the repertoire. The period is the turn of the century, and the music takes the form of contemporary light-hearted waltzes by the Cuban composer Lecuona. Four sisters love each other dearly, but there are painful undercurrents in their relationships – for example, one sister is deeply in love, but cannot marry the man because, according to the Spanish and Cuban custom of the time, the eldest sister must marry first. *La Diva* was very different in style, but showed the same sensitivity. In this, Mendez had Alicia Alonso dance mainly with her hands, suggesting the very personal and expressive gestures of Maria Callas.

Alicia Alonso and Orlando Salgado in one of the tautly erotic duets in Cuban National Ballet's production of Carmen, *choreography by Alberto Alonso.*

Iván Tenorio has gradually developed a flair for strong dramatic ballets, with the drama treated in a bold, formal manner. In *Hamlet*, he presented the action of the Shakespeare play in a simplified and much-condensed manner, using only the main characters, but retaining Shakespeare's characterization as well as his complex themes. Characteristically, Tenorio made no attempt to spread the ballet out over a complete evening, in the manner popularized in the West by Lavrovsky's *Romeo and Juliet*.

Alberto Alonso studied African ritual dances (with their gods and goddesses) in Nigeria, and also their survival in Cuba. In *O-Ye-Ye-O*, he created an Afro-Cuban version of Perrot's ballet for four cosmopolitan ballerinas, *Le Pas de quatre*: it is a delight to see the noble and elegant artist Josefina Mendez interpreting the floating dance-images of Yemaya, goddess of the sea, which fuse Afro-Cuban movements and ballet technique. Caridad Martinez looks impudently seductive as Ochun (goddess of love) while Mirta Plá is quick and vibrant as Oya, goddess of wind and lightness. Other dancers, tackling the same roles, interpret them with nuances of their own, while retaining the overall quality.

Gustavo Herrera took some years to reach the point where he was able to carry off his ambitious ballet *Electra Garrigó*, with its Cuban interpretation of the ancient Greek myth. Sexual symbolism was stressed not only in the dancing of Clytemnestra (created by Loipa Araújo) and Electra (created by Ofelia Gonzales), but also in the sets by Ricardo Reimana – the stage dominated by a giant papaya with a glowing red core.

The choreographers are much helped by the fact that they can call on the vibrant talents of dancers such as these, and there are a number of others, each with a strongly etched personality. Lazaro Carreño, for example, was quite splendid as Hamlet; and Marta García, Amparo Brito, Andres Williams, Fernando Jhones and Orlando Salgado are no less individual and expressive. Jorge Esquivel danced superbly with the company for years and partnered Alicia Alonso with skill and artistry. Then he left to join the Camagüey Ballet directed by Alicia Alonso's ex-husband, Fernando Alonso. Diaghilev had at his disposal a galaxy of talent up to the outbreak of the First World War, and Tudor was able to use an equally diverse group of remarkable artists in the golden age of Ballet Theatre in the Forties. For the full development of their talents, choreographers need such dancers.

Training is under the expert supervision of the remarkable teacher Laura Alonso, daughter of Alicia Alonso, and the leading dancers take part in training and coaching. Now there is no prejudice among Cuban parents about having their boys trained in ballet; rather, it is considered a great honour to be chosen for the school. Indeed, ballet is intensely popular among Cubans, reaching a very wide public, while maintaining the highest standards and never 'playing down'.

CHAPTER NINETEEN

Jiří Kylián and The Netherlands Dance Theatre

Jiří Kylián was born in Czechoslovakia, trained in ballet at the Prague Conservatoire, then came to London on a scholarship, and trained at the Royal Ballet School. In 1968, he joined the Stuttgart Ballet where, in the stimulating atmosphere of this company and encouraged by Cranko, he gained rapidly in maturity as he quickly created a series of ballets. Occasionally he worked for the Netherlands Dance Theatre, and in 1975 became artistic director of this company. His work as choreographer and director was so remarkable that he quite transformed the NDT, making it unlike any other and always able to cope superbly with the highly original ballets he created for it. Like Tudor (to whom he showed great affinity), he demanded a high degree of skill in classical ballet technique from his dancers, so that they could do justice to his challenging and highly expressive dance-images. American modern dance had some influence on him, and he was able to take advantage of the

Sinfonietta, *with Jiří Kylián using Leoŝ Janáček's music to evoke his beloved Czechoslovakia in light-hearted nostalgic mood, with quick-footed choreography suggesting Czech national dances. Netherlands Dance Theatre.*

fact that the American male dancers who joined his company had usually been trained in both ballet and modern dance. However, this was only one of a number of influences, which included Czech folk dances and folk music and the music of Czech composers.

Just as Tudor had been influenced by Fokine, Kylián was influenced by Tudor – indeed, he dedicated his ballet *Overgrown Path* to him – but he developed a style of his own and carved out his own path. One striking quality of his early choreography was his use of blocks of dancers, moving them about the stage with great skill. There was conflict between these blocks of dancers, and also between soloists who emerged from them from time to time; but there were also episodes full of lyricism. These qualities emerged very clearly in *Sinfonietta*, a ballet which means a great deal to him. It is dedicated to his mother, it uses music by the Czech composer Leoš Janáček, and it carries an intense charge of emotion – that of a Czech living in exile from his beloved country. Kylián did incorporate some short solos, but the main emphasis was on group dancing, used by him with new and very personal expressiveness.

In *Svadebka* (Russian for 'a little marriage'), Kylián achieved something one would have thought impossible: a new version of the Nijinska ballet *Les Noces* which, in some ways, was better than the original. Studying Stravinsky's score very carefully, he discovered – in the words assigned to the chorus – aspects of the ballet that had not been developed by Nijinska's choreography. He realized, in particular, the mutual dislike of the bride and groom – brought together by matchmakers in an arranged marriage, according to ancient Russian peasant custom. In Nijinska's version, the bride and groom hardly

LEFT Svadebka – *Jiří Kylián's re-interpretation of* Les Noces, *using the original Stravinsky music. Bride and groom are brought together by the pressure of tradition. Netherlands Dance Theatre.*
BELOW *In Jiří Kylián's* Stamping Ground, *inspired by Australian aboriginal dancing, two artists perform dance-images suggesting animal movements, but with their own expressive language. Netherlands Dance Theatre.*

dance at all: the solo dancing is done by two people emerging from the group, for no apparent reason. In *Svadebka*, the matchmakers, the fathers and mothers of the bride and groom, and the group dancers are all given dance-images which show them gradually bringing the bride and groom together, drawing on the power of long-established tradition. As the ballet draws to a close, their dancing shows them abandoning their mutual dislike and they walk out to consummate the marriage in the marriage bed, in a joyous ending which exactly reflects the mood of the music.

Touring with his company in Australia, Kylián attended a gathering of aborigines from all over Australia. The people of different tribes spoke different languages, but they communicated in dance, and Kylián was deeply impressed by their dances – containing many kinds of stamping, close imitation of animals and birds, and religious symbolism. He distilled what he saw into yet another choreographic masterpiece: *Stamping Ground*. In his choreography, he took care not to use any actual aboriginal steps, for he knew that these are the property of the individuals, but he caught the aboriginal flavour admirably in dance-images of extraordinary complexity. (Tudor said of Kylián that he did all sorts of things that *he* had wanted to do, but had never got around to.) One delightful aspect of this ballet is that it is very funny: Kylián treated the dances of the aborigines with the greatest respect, but when he created a ballet inspired by them, he did it in his own way.

Kylián was strongly attracted to the Colette–Ravel opera *L'Enfant et les sortilèges* (*The Child and the Spells*), both by its theme and its music.

Netherlands Dance Theatre performing L'Enfant et les Sortilèges, *the Colette-Ravel fantasy-opera transformed into a ballet by Jiří Kylián. The boy (Marley Knoben) cowers behind the dancing armchair.*

Colette had been taught by her mother, a remarkable woman, to appreciate nature, and much the same had happened to Kylián; in fact, he dedicated his ballet to his mother. He delighted in having the music sung by invisible singers and showing the opera taking shape on stage as performed by dancers, for he knew that the possibilities for movement open to singers are strictly limited, since they need their breath for singing. The Kylián version was more than a ballet added to an opera: something new and fascinating emerged from this fusion of arts.

Ravel planned the opera as a musical comedy, and most of the first scene has music belonging to that world, showing the influence of jazz. Being deeply musical, Kylián created choreography for the first scene which was the equivalent of the music: the bad-tempered boy, indifferent to nature, was strongly and convincingly projected by Marley Knoben, and some of the action was farcical. Then, towards the end of the first scene, the quality of the choreography changed in a magical way, in harmony with the change in the style of Ravel's music – which began to show his superb flair for orchestration and his lyricism.

It was when the two cats (Catherine Allard and Nacho Duato) attacked the boy with sinuous feline movements that the ballet took off, showing Kylián's delightful sense of humour. This scene acted as a bridge to the magic of the scene in the garden, where every dance-image has its own quality (suited to the creature performing it) and yet bears the unmistakable stamp of Kylián. The bird, for example, danced on *pointe* with elegant, flowing arm movements which caused her wings (of light blue cloth) to float behind her; the female dragon-fly, also on *pointe*, danced with delicate menace, moving her legs through fascinating curves. Other animals (such as the frogs and the squirrel) danced in unblocked ballet shoes.

Like Rambert and Alonso, Kylián takes care to foster the development of choreographers, who get a chance to develop their creative powers working with the 'youth' company. Here the dancers are highly trained and fully professional, but have to be very good indeed if they are to graduate to the main company.

In 1987, Kylián and his dancers had the joy of moving to the new Dance Theatre on the Spui, in the middle of The Hague, which had been purpose-built for dance – thus establishing an important precedent, as well as providing the Netherlands Dance Theatre with ideal facilities.

Holland is a small country, but it supports an amazing variety of ballet. Apart from NDT, there is also the National Ballet, a big company with a very extensive repertoire.

CHAPTER TWENTY

South Africa, Canada and Australia

South Africa

Two of the finest artists who worked at the Ballet Club before the Second World War came from South Africa. Maude Lloyd was Tudor's first leading dancer, and remained devoted to him. Frank Staff, however, took his own line. Technically, he developed in a remarkable way; he was, for example, capable of performing triple *tours en l'air*. Younger than Ashton and Tudor, he did not begin his choreographic career until 1939 when he was 21. Like them he was deeply affected by the remarkably stimulating atmosphere maintained by Marie Rambert, and his first ballet, *Czernyana* (1939), a suite of light-hearted dances to the music of Czerny piano exercises, was a highly professional work which Rambert was glad to add to her repertoire.

With his second ballet, *Peter and the Wolf* (1940), he established himself as a highly talented choreographer with a delightful sense of humour and a very individual approach. What gave *Peter and the Wolf*, with its imaginative scenery and costumes, such charm and such enduring appeal was that it resembled the piece by Prokofiev on which it was based: it seemed childish – the sort of ballet a child might create – when, in fact, it was highly sophisticated, demanding remarkable dancers with a strong sense of style. Frank Staff made sure that all these demands were met, and for many years it was one of the most popular ballets in the Rambert repertoire.

The designer Guy Sheppard more than met these demands with his imagination and originality. For his sets, he employed the same sort of props that a child might use while playing – step-ladders, mops, a plank, a very small pool placed on the stage and so on – and his costumes were equally charming and witty. Staff made use of the

Peter and the Wolf, *created by Frank Staff in 1940 and re-staged by him for the CAPAB Ballet, Cape Town. Carolé Wilson is the Duck, Nicholas van der Merwe the Wolf.*

material provided by Sheppard, together with the talents of the dancers, with skill and inventiveness. Some of his effects were broadly farcical, such as the antics of the hunters; others were subtle and humorous.

After the war, a remarkable group of South African dancers came to London and made a fine contribution to British ballet for many years. They included Nadia Nerina (for whom Ashton created the leading role of Lise in *La Fille mal gardée*), the future choreographers John Cranko and Alfred Rodrigues, David Poole, Maryon Lane, Patricia Miller, Vyvyan Lorayne, Desmond Doyle, Deanne Bergsma, Johaar Mosaval and Monica Mason. Two other remarkable dancers who arrived in Britain from southern Africa were Dianne Richards (from what is now Zambia) who became a ballerina in the London Festival Ballet, and Merle Park (from what is now Zimbabwe) who became a ballerina in the Royal Ballet and, subsequently, the director of the Royal Ballet School.

A number of these artists had been trained by the fine South African teacher, Dulcie Howes, who had herself been trained in London in the Twenties, and then danced with the Pavlova company. She returned to South Africa where she established the University of Cape Town School of Ballet in 1934. After the war, the performing group of this school, the University of Cape Town Ballet (later called CAPAB), became a professional company, directed by Dulcie Howes. In 1959, after years of dancing in British companies, David Poole joined it and did fine work as its ballet master.

After Frank Staff returned to South Africa in 1953, he worked for this and other South African companies, reviving his London ballets (notably *Peter and the Wolf*, which became a popular favourite), and also creating a number of new ballets, including *Transfigured Night* (using the same Schönberg music that Tudor had used for *Pillar of Fire*) and the Prokofiev *Romeo and Juliet*. His untimely death in 1971, at the age of 53, was serious blow to South African ballet.

The PACT (Performing Arts Council of the Transvaal) Ballet, founded in Johannesburg in 1963, and with Faith de Villiers as artistic director from 1964, has always had a close relationship with the Royal Ballet, which sent some of its best dancers to guest with it.

South African dancers, now able to make a career in their own country, in these and other companies, have maintained the fine standard of polished professionalism which had been characteristic of South African ballet for decades.

Monica Mason dancing the title role of Fokine's The Firebird, *wearing the relatively conventional costume designed by Natalia Goncharova for Diaghilev in 1926. Royal Ballet at Covent Garden, 1980.*

Merle Park dancing with Nureyev a pas de deux *from the Petipa ballet* Le Corsaire. *Royal Ballet at Covent Garden, c. 1970.*

Canada

Canada is the second largest country in the world; but its population is mainly concentrated in a very long (and relatively narrow) strip near the border with the United States. This great distance had led to the emergence of three major companies, in three cities. Each has its distinctive history, and has developed in its own way, even though each has had to pursue the same policy of spending much of the year on tour, taking in American cities as well as Canadian ones.

Canada began to produce outstanding dancers long before there were any professional companies in Canada. The dancers were trained in Vancouver, on the Pacific coast, where there were several fine Canadian and Russian teachers. June Roper (herself trained by Olga Preobrazhenskaya in Paris) taught several dancers who later entered the De Basil Ballets Russes; one of them, who took the name Alexandra Denisova, was a leading soloist. Lois Smith, a superb artist, became Canada's first homegrown ballerina. Robert Lindgren, who danced with the Denham Ballet Russe, and the New York City Ballet, became director of a ballet school and a regional ballet company in North Carolina. Lynn Seymour became a star of the Royal Ballet.

The oldest of the Canadian companies is the Royal Winnipeg. This company became fully professional in 1949, and was granted a royal charter by Queen Elizabeth in 1953 – three years before the Sadler's Wells Ballet was given this honour. Under the direction of Arnold Spohr, it developed on much the same lines as the Denham Ballet Russe company – touring widely with a similar repertoire of popular one-act ballets. Spohr did his best to foster the work of Canadian choreographers, but – like the directors of the other companies in the country – he had difficulty in staging Canadian ballets that then stood the test of time. One young Royal Winnipeg dancer, Evelyn Hart, did achieve fame through winning an international ballet competition. The presence in the company of this exceptionally talented artist made it possible for him to commission his Russian ballet mistress Galina Yordanovich to stage a successful production of *Swan Lake* in 1987. Profiting from the fact that she had trained the dancers of the company in the Russian 'school', she was able to meet Spohr's imaginative request for a relatively traditional version, paying due respect to Ivanov's choreography in the 'swan' acts. She managed to create a fine atmosphere, even though the fact that the company had only twenty-six dancers gave her severe problems. The production gained much from the lighting of Nicholas Cernovich – one of the world's greatest lighting designers – and from the stage designs of Peter Farmer.

The National Ballet of Canada came into existence in 1951 when a group of Toronto citizens invited Celia Franca – who had started with the Ballet Club under Rambert and Tudor, and then danced with the Sadler's Wells Ballet – to establish a company in that city. Modelling it mainly on Sadler's Wells, she worked with great determination, against enormous odds. Funds were short, and almost all the young dancers lacked stage experience; fortunately, she was able to take on Lois Smith and her husband David Adams, who did have stage experience – though it was in musicals and operettas, there being no ballet company in Vancouver.

Franca was obsessed with the Tudor ballet *Jardin aux lilas* (in which she had danced the role of the ex-mistress, rehearsed by Tudor and Laing) and bravely staged this for the NBC in its second season, persuading Tudor and Laing to fill in gaps and give the ballet a final polish. The great success of this ballet encouraged her to establish a group of Tudor ballets in the repertoire (notably *Dark Elegies* and *Gala Performance*). Franca herself, Lois Smith and David Adams lent a fine quality to these productions, and together they helped the whole company to mature.

In 1983, Erik Bruhn became the company's artistic director. He expanded the repertoire, raised the standard of dancing and encouraged dancers who had left the NBC to return. His death in 1986 was a severe blow to the company. But it was much stimulated by the appointment of Glen Tetley in 1987 as artistic associate. As a choreographer, he had been going through a bad patch, after the great success of his early ballets; but he delighted in settling down with the National Ballet of Canada, and celebrated his appointment by creating a new ballet well suited to his complex temperament. This was *La Ronde*, based on the cynical play by Arthur Schnitzler which revealed the loveless sensuality and moral decadence evident in the lives of the Viennese late in the 19th century. He had to create a chain of ten *pas de deux*, linking together sexual encounters of ten very different people, and tackled this choreographic problem with skill and confidence, guiding the dancers to project the various characters

The National Ballet of Canada in La Ronde, *created for the company by Glen Tetley in 1987. The dancers are John Alleyne and Ronda Nychka.*

Evelyn Hart in the 'Black Swan' pas de deux *– adapted from the* pas de deux *of Odile and Prince Siegfried in Act III of* Swan Lake. *Royal Winnipeg Ballet.*

and moods, and paying subtle tribute to Tudor's ballet *Dim Lustre*.

Les Grands Ballets Canadiens, performing mainly in Quebec, began life in Montreal in a very unusual way – as a television ballet company. This had choreography by Ludmilla Chiriaeff, who had been trained in Berlin by the Russian teacher Alexandra Nicolaeva, and then danced in various European companies. Under her direction, the company established a clear French-Canadian flavour, offering opportunities to numerous resident dancers as well as those from outside Quebec. Ludmilla Chiriaeff's television experience was a great help when she collaborated with Norman McClaren on the superb film ballet *Pas de deux*. The company gained much from the contributions by the outstanding American lighting designer Nicholas Cernovich, and from the dancing of the Swedish ballerina Annette av Paul – who had been rehearsed by Tudor in Stockholm, and chose to dance the role of Caroline in *Jardin aux lilas* for her farewell performance in 1984. In 1987, she became founder-director of a new ballet company in Vancouver.

Marilyn Jones, prima ballerina of the Australian Ballet from 1966 to her retirement, dances Odette in Swan Lake, *Act II, for this company. She is partnered by Jonathon Kelly as Prince Siegfried.*

Australia

Before the Second World War, Australia was so remote from Europe that ballet remained almost unknown there. In fact, the first great Australian dancer Robert Helpmann had to travel to London to establish his career.

When the De Basil Ballets Russes company toured Australia in 1939, the Czech soloist Edouard Borovansky stayed behind – establishing first a school and then, in 1942, the Borovansky Ballet. This carried on the Ballets Russes tradition with productions such as *Giselle, Coppélia, Le Carnaval* (Fokine) and *Le Beau Danube*, together with ballets by Borovansky and others. The company had a hard time, for performances could only be given in the very small number of large cities, and had to disband from time to time.

Peggy van Praagh was brought in as director after Borovansky's death in 1959, but increasing costs forced the final disbanding of the company a year later. The next major step forward in Australian ballet was the foundation of the Australian Ballet in 1962, with Peggy van Praagh as director; she saved what was best of the work of the Borovansky Ballet, and brought into the company some of the fine dancers who were emerging from Australian ballet schools.

In 1969, Van Praagh finally succeeded in giving substance to her dream of bringing Tudor to Australia to stage ballets for the company. The Australian dancers did well in *Pillar of Fire*, rehearsed by Tudor and Laing – with Kathleen Geldard making a brave attempt at Hagar. Gailene Stock did wonders with a strange role in Tudor's new Haitian ballet *The Divine Horsemen*; however, the remoteness of the voodoo theme of the ballet and the lack of time available to Tudor to mould the dancers defeated this project.

Robert Helpmann – who had become co-director with Peggy van Praagh in 1965 – staged for the company his finest ballet *Hamlet*, which he had created for the Sadler's Wells Ballet in 1942. In effect, this was a mime play, showing the events of Hamlet's life as remembered by him in a confused way as he lay dying. Helpmann himself had given a superb performance of the central role at the world première in London, and so did Nureyev when he took over this role (as guest artist) at the Australian première in 1970.

Marilyn Jones now emerged as the company's glorious prima ballerina, giving poetic beauty to the classics and to such modern roles as Juliet in the Cranko version of *Romeo and Juliet*, as well as to the leading roles of ballets by Australian choreographers. Lucette Aldous, returning from

Britain, also shone. By now, so many good dancers were emerging from Australian ballet schools that the company could be very selective.

Illness forced Peggy van Praagh to abandon her direction of the company in 1979. When Marilyn Jones took over, she found herself faced with seemingly insoluble problems. Fortunately, Maina Gielgud, who became artistic director in 1983, had the right qualities, and under her, the company flourished. She brought in Jiří Kylián's delectable comedy *Symphony in D* and his complex *Forgotten Land*, as well as Maurice Béjart's *Songs of a Wayfarer*. Drawing on her extensive experience in Europe, she staged new productions of *Giselle* and *Sleeping Beauty* – bringing the latter to Covent Garden for a season in the summer of 1988, the year in which Australia celebrated the bicentennial of the arrival of the 'first fleet' of convict settlers to Australia.

Modern dance also has a presence in Australia. After the disbanding of the Dance–Drama Group in 1938 in London – where Margaret Barr managed to keep it in existence for a period in the later Thirties, after leaving Dartington Hall – she returned to Australia, and was a pioneer in establishing modern dance there.

In Britain, Australia's bicentennial was celebrated by the presentation in Portsmouth (from where the 'first fleet' embarked in 1787) of a remarkable new work by Kai Tai Chan, director of the One Extra Company – which has its own approach to modern dance, influenced by Kai Tai Chan's roots in both East and West. (Ethnically Chinese, he had emigrated to Australia from Malaysia twenty years earlier.) His work *The Shrew* took its theme from Shakespeare's play *The Taming of the Shrew*, but he gave it a fresh interpretation. Most of the action took place in China under the Qing dynasty, and he made superb use of Chinese theatrical traditions – for example, cladding his dancers in gorgeous robes and showing women with bound feet. However, he used *pointe* shoes as an equivalent for the bound feet, and drew a parallel between the subjection of Chinese women (symbolized by their bound feet) and the problems faced by women in a modern Western society.

In Forgotten Land *Jiří Kylián's semi-abstract choreography, to music by Benjamin Britten, suggests the sea and exile from a beloved homeland. (L to r) Ulrike Lytton, Paul de Masson. Australian Ballet.*

CHAPTER TWENTY-ONE

China and Japan

China

The flowering of Chinese ballet after a decade in which it suffered terribly under Jiang Qing – Mao Tse-Tung's wife who, as one of the 'Gang of Four', took a special interest in ballet – is one of the most remarkable events in the history of ballet, showing the extraordinary Chinese flair for ballet and their amazing resilience.

Dai Ai-Lian was given the task of establishing the Central Ballet School and the Central Ballet Company in Beijing after the foundation of the People's Republic in 1949, and she was exactly the right person for this task. Born in Trinidad of Chinese parents, she had come to London to train as a dancer during the golden age of British ballet in the Thirties. After studying with Anton Dolin, and with Rambert and Tudor at the Rambert school, she began to create beautifully structured and expressive solo dances in a Chinese style that she developed from her study of Chinese painting and sculpture. For six months, she trained at Dartington Hall in Devon in the Jooss–Leeder style of modern dance; then she went to Shanghai, and began to teach ballet. She also made trips to remote parts of China to study the exquisite dances of the minority nationalities, preserving ancient traditions.

In the early Fifties, she worked with energy and imagination on the development of ballet in Beijing. The dancers made fine progress in mastering a style that was remote in many ways from what was common in Chinese dance – although traditional Chinese theatre includes soaring leaps, apparently defying gravity, which are much the

The Flying Apsaras, *with choreography by Dai Ai-Lian: a reconstruction of dancing depicted in ancient cave paintings, and performed by Dai Yisun and Yang Jun. Central Song and Dance Ensemble.*

ABOVE *The third* pas de deux *of* Four Romantic Pieces, *choreographed by Maria Fay for the Central Ballet of China in 1984. Love in maturity, interpreted by Wang Pingping and her partner Zhou Weikang.*

same as the leaps of ballet.

Dai Ai-Lian made a remarkable contribution to Chinese dance in 1956 by reconstructing an ancient style of dancing, portrayed in frescoes on the walls of the Dun Huang caves, far out on the Silk Road. The painted dancers manipulated long lengths of silk as they danced, holding them in the middle and causing them to whirl in a magical way, and Dai Ai-Lian reproduced these same patterns in *The Flying Apsaras*. She showed her extraordinary flair for construction when she made the solo into a *pas de deux*, with the two curving lengths of silk creating fascinating patterns as they interwove in space around the dancers. Understandably, the *pas de deux* became immensely popular in China.

The arrival, in 1957, of a group of Soviet teachers led by the former head of the Kirov Ballet, Pyotr Gusev, had complex results. The Chinese dancers profited from being taught the Russian 'school', as systematized by Vaganova, and they were given the chance of dancing in such classics as *Swan Lake*. But the development of Chinese choreography was badly distorted, since the young choreographers were taught by Gusev to create full-length ballets in a very conventional, 'overstuffed' way, taking no account of the great achievements in ballet in the 20th century. After the sudden departure of the Soviets in 1960, Chinese choreographers, working in teams, did their best to create two ballets with Chinese themes, *The Red Detachment of Women* and *The White-Haired Girl*, which both included interesting scenes, and had some merit.

Dai Ai-Lian and the best Chinese dancers were treated very cruelly by Jiang Qing, who sent them

RIGHT The Maid of the Sea, *based on a Chinese legend, with choreography by Li Chengxiang, Wang Shiqi and Li Chenglian. Dancers in the group represent seaweed. Central Ballet of China.*

out to work on farms. Jiang also made sure that only *The Red Detachment of Women* and *The White-Haired Girl* were performed, and that the training of the remaining dancers was confined to the big steps used in these two ballets. Chinese ballet stagnated for a decade, and traditions of classical dancing were almost lost.

After the arrest of the 'Gang of Four' in 1976 and the end of the Cultural Revolution, Dai Ai-Lian and the exiled dancers returned to the ballet world. Recovery was slow at first – the dancers had suffered terribly in the previous ten years – but became faster and faster. The young dancers emerging from the school showed superb quality, aided by a series of fine teachers whom Dai Ai-Lian – now adviser to the Central Ballet School and the Central Ballet Company, and making regular visits to the West – arranged to be invited to work in Beijing. She also arranged for producers to stage significant modern ballets such as Balanchine's *Serenade*, and for choreographers to restage their best works.

She struck gold when she invited Maria Fay to come and teach in Beijing, for the Ministry of Culture asked Fay, in addition to her daily company classes, to take in hand a very promising group of fifteen young dancers, teaching them how to cope with Western choreography. The result was *Four Romantic Pieces*: the first ballet created by a Western choreographer for Chinese dancers, one that demonstrated their extraordinary capacity for evoking nuances of mood and emotion, as well as their ability to dance with grace, elegance and beautiful line. Four successive *pas de deux* (danced by four couples) were blended with group dances, to show four stages in the life

LEFT *The Tokyo Ballet dancing Béjart's* The Kabuki, 47 Samurai *(1986).*

of a woman – from childish innocence and mischievous adolescence to mature love and, finally, death. This ballet – together with the work of a continuing influx of teachers and choreographers from the West – helps Chinese dancers to stand up to comparison with any others in the world.

Japan

When Pavlova visited Japan for the first time in 1922, she made a tremendous impression, and a number of ballet schools were started – first with *emigré* Russian teachers, and then with Soviet teachers. After the Second World War, Japanese companies were formed, using dancers trained in Japan as well as those who had gone to Western countries to train.

The Japanese companies had a pattern of organization rather like that of the Ballet Club in London in the Thirties: the dancers were unpaid, and had to take another job during the day to earn a living. But they suffered from performing only at long intervals, for very short seasons. Also, the directors of the companies found it impossible to maintain a repertoire of good modern ballets brought in from the West: the Japanese were interested only in seeing the latest productions.

Fortunately, there is one company, the Tokyo Ballet, which has succeeded in establishing itself as truly professional and persistent. It has been strongly influenced by Soviet ballet, and has had little success encouraging Japanese choreographers. On the other hand, Maurice Béjart made a deep impression with *The Kabuki, 47 Samurai*, in which he adapted Kabuki ideas with great skill, using as his principal dancer a fine artist from the Paris Opéra Ballet who had a Vietnamese father and a French mother: Eric Vu-An. The ballet is based on a true Japanese story, already adapted as a Kabuki drama, and Béjart showed a capacity for precise observation, notably in his presentation of the finale – the

RIGHT *The Noh piece* Kinuta, *performed by the Nanjo-Okumura Noh Troupe, 1983. The Japanese modern-dance style Butoh, as danced by Kazuo Ohno, owes much to ancient Noh traditions.*

traditional suicide of the forty-seven samurai, with all the correct rituals. The *danseuses* wore Japanese kimonos at first, but stripped them off to dance in all-over tights to show a change in atmosphere. Here was a French choreographer, much influenced by the East, using Japanese dancers to interpret a Japanese theme, with his characteristic expressionism and love of spectacle – qualities also much favoured in Kabuki, and well appreciated by Japanese dancers and audiences.

One very strange and impressive style of modern dance – Butoh, which is much influenced by the ancient, slow-moving Japanese Noh dance-drama – has been performed by Kazuo Ohno, starting in the Thirties. Even when he was in his eighties, he continued to create an impressive effect as he danced.

CHAPTER TWENTY-TWO

Cosmopolitan Superstars

Erik Bruhn

Erik Bruhn was born in Copenhagen, trained at the school of the Royal Danish Ballet and, soon after joining the company, established himself as the finest of the male dancers – in a company where traditions of male dancing had been strongly preserved right through the many years of decadence in the second half of the 19th century, because of the surviving influence of Bournonville. Anxious to retain artists like Bruhn – who might be expected to leave to star in the great capital cities of the world – the management of the company had established a system whereby Danish dancers have the freedom to dance outside Denmark while still remaining members of the company and dancing regularly with it. Bruhn began to dance abroad in 1947 – the same year that he entered the company – and continued to do so while remaining one of the strengths of the Royal Danish Ballet, and gaining much from the teaching of Vera Volkova.

Becoming a cosmopolitan superstar, he guested with American Ballet Theatre, the New York City Ballet, the Royal Ballet in London, the Australian Ballet, the Royal Swedish Ballet, the Harkness Ballet, the Paris Opéra Ballet and several other companies. He was acclaimed in the Soviet Union when he toured there with American Ballet Theatre. Though he and Nureyev could hardly have been more different in temperament, they became close friends. In 1966 Bruhn danced with another cosmopolitan superstar, Carla Fracci, with Bruhn working as guest artist and producer for the Rome Opera Ballet.

As a dancer he was distinguished by the impeccable classical purity and nobility of his style which became completely international, much influenced by the Russian 'school' as exemplified in the dancing of Nureyev; but he kept his own type of elegance. He confined himself almost entirely to the romantic roles of the international repertoire, to which his style of dancing was attuned: James in *La Sylphide*, Albrecht in *Giselle*, Spectre in *Le Spectre de la rose*, the male role in *Les Sylphides*, Romeo in Ashton's version of *Romeo and Juliet*, and so on. He staged *La Sylphide* for the National Ballet of Canada in 1964 (dancing the role of James at the première), preparing the way for his appointment as director of the company in 1983, near the end of his life.

OPPOSITE *Erik Bruhn as Prince Siegfried in* Swan Lake. *By temperament he was ideally suited to such roles, being a true* danseur noble.
LEFT *Erik Bruhn as Prince Siegfried – one of his finest roles – with Nadia Nerina as Odette in* Swan Lake, *Act II. Royal Ballet, 1962.*
BELOW *In* Romeo and Juliet *two cosmopolitan superstars, Erik Bruhn and Carla Fracci, join forces as they dance romantic roles for which they are both ideally suited. New York, 1967.*

Carla Fracci

It was no accident that two of the cosmopolitan superstars of the Romantic ballet were Italian: generations of Italian dancers – including members of the Viganò family – had already toured Europe, establishing the fine quality of Italian teaching and the Italian flair for dancing. The male dancers were often choreographers as well.

It was Italian superstars who became the idols of the public in St Petersburg towards the end of the 19th century; indeed, they came to take leading roles in the new ballets, Russians being considered unsuited to such roles because technically the Italians were in advance of them. Even Odette–Odile, heroine of that very Russian ballet *Swan Lake*, was created by an Italian superstar, Pierina Legnani. It was the same in Paris: imported Italian stars such as Giuseppina Bozacchi (first exponent of Swanilda in *Coppélia*) and Carlotta Zambelli danced the leading roles.

Carla Fracci re-established, in the 20th century, the tradition of these Italian stars. Born in Milan, she trained at the ballet school of La Scala, joined the company and showed such fantastic talent that it was not long before she was what in other countries would be called a 'prima ballerina'. With her great beauty, her charm, her strong technique and her delightful and strongly etched personality, she established herself as perfect for romantic roles. Dancing the role of the Italian ballerina in Anton Dolin's reconstruction of Perrot's ballet *Le Pas de quatre*, she brought to life Dolin's rather unimaginative choreography for the Cerrito role. In fact she is very different from Cerrito in temperament: Cerrito was tempestuous, strongly dramatic and erotic, whereas Fracci is lyrical and elegant.

In 1960, when she was only 24, she began to establish herself as a cosmopolitan superstar, performing Giselle as guest artist with London's Festival Ballet. From that time she began to appear as guest artist in many companies, and tackled a wide variety of roles, including the leading ones in all the 19th-century 'classics': *Swan Lake*, *The Sleeping Beauty*, *La Fille mal gardée*, *Coppélia*. For some years, in the Sixties, she danced regularly for American Ballet Theatre, thus establishing a pattern for other cosmopolitan superstars: they like to perform regularly with one company but usually move on after a few years.

Fracci danced the role created by Markova in Tudor's one-act version of *Romeo and Juliet*, and also in the versions of the Prokofiev ballet by Cranko and Nureyev. Continually widening her range, she danced dramatic roles such as Desdemona in José Limon's ballet *The Moor's Pavane* (based on American modern dance). In Italy, Fracci is revered as a goddess: she has become the supreme Italian dancer of her time.

Rudolf Nureyev

Nureyev was the first of the great Soviet dancers to defect in order to achieve wider opportunities for his dancing. Born in 1938, he had been trained by the great teacher Alexander Pushkin in Leningrad, at the school attached to the Kirov Ballet (the Vaganova Choreographic Academy), and was one of the best young male dancers in the Soviet Union. In 1961, he defected from the Kirov in Paris, and was invited to London for a gala by

Carla Fracci looking sultry and amorous as Zobeide in Schéhérazade. *In this role Fokine made extensive use of his own highly concentrated style of mime, and Fracci found in it fine opportunities.*

Margot Fonteyn – thus establishing a superb partnership which was to last for many years, and which gave Fonteyn (whose dancing had begun to look lack-lustre) a new vitality.

Nureyev achieved such fame that he was able to do what he liked. Convinced that he thrived on a pattern of work which would have nearly killed any other dancer, he performed every night in full-length ballets staged by himself, even taking over both the London Festival Ballet and the Ballet-Théâtre de Nancy for successive seasons in London. His ambition was boundless, and he did not seem worried by the fact that, on first nights, his own performance suffered because of his concern to oversee the ballet as a whole. He danced in scores of roles, guesting with a great many companies around the world, and achieved fame such as no male dancer had enjoyed since Nijinsky. When he first danced the role of Petrushka with the Royal Ballet, he made the

Nureyev as Petrushka, dancing with Ballet Théâtre Français de Nancy at the Edinburgh Festival, 1987.

mistake of changing the choreography; it was only years later that he came to terms with Fokine's wonderfully expressive dance-images, and danced them superbly, so that the ballet sprang to life. Here he showed himself taking up the mantle of Nijinsky, and he did the same when he danced the faun in *L'Après-midi d'un faune*, with the Fokine choreography preserved by the Ballet Rambert – though he did not adopt the very strange walk created by Nijinsky.

He was splendid as the murderous teacher in Flemming Flindt's ballet *The Lesson*, but in technically exacting roles such as Albrecht in *Giselle*, he was afflicted by problems of technique as he grew older. Such was his obsession for dance that it did not seem to bother him that, by continuing to appear in such roles, he obscured the memory of his glorious achievements in them at earlier stages of his career.

One of his most striking attributes is his open-minded attitude to forms of dance remote from ballet. For twenty years, he delighted in dancing in works by Martha Graham – and she was no less delighted to have him in her works. Indeed, he took part in a major retrospective season in November 1987 at the Center Theater in New York – dancing the role of the Revivalist in *Appalachian Spring*. He has also been happy to dance in Paul Taylor's *Aureole*. When creating full-length spectacular ballets, he has remained deeply influenced by his youth in the Soviet Union; but he is also a cosmopolitan citizen of the world, with a keen and sensitive understanding of a wide diversity of developments in ballet and modern dance in the West. Like Pavlova – whose obsession with dancing was comparable to his – he is a fascinating bundle of contradictions.

In 1983, when he took over the very challenging

LEFT *Nureyev performing a leap as Prince Charming in* The Sleeping Beauty. *Royal Ballet at Covent Garden.*
OVERLEAF LEFT *Natalia Makarova as a regal, mature Tatiana in Cranko's* Onegin, *Act III, staged for London Festival Ballet by Stuttgart Ballet's choreologist/ballet mistress Georgette Tsinguirides. Michael Pink (Prince Gremin) partners Makarova (1985).*

post of director of the Paris Opéra Ballet – within which he could dance as often as he liked – he made sure that his contract gave him three months each year when he was free to dance as guest artist with other companies. Like Pavlova, he was prepared to go almost anywhere to dance, but he did not allow his obsession with dancing to interfere with his magnificent work as director.

Inevitably, the tremendous strain on his body took its toll, but he continued to dance almost as often as before. Although as he approached and passed the age of 50 he still took on a variety of roles, he is seen at his best in those suited to his technique at this stage of his career.

Nureyev as Prince Siegfried and Natalia Makarova as Odile in the 'Black Swan' pas de deux. *BBC TV, 1 January 1971 – soon after Makarova's defection from the Kirov Ballet in London.*
OVERLEAF RIGHT *Mikhail Baryshnikov in the title role of the Fokine ballet* Le Spectre de la rose, *making his first appearance through the window.*

Natalia Makarova

The 21-year-old Natalia Makarova had established herself as the most promising of the rising young ballerinas of the Kirov Ballet when the company came to the West in 1961. She owed much to the careful teaching of two great Kirov teachers, Tatiana Vecheslova and Natalia Dudinskaya. With Vecheslova, she found poetic expressiveness, while Dudinskaya, herself a dancer of superb technical accomplishments, helped her to achieve a marvellous technique.

The director of the company, Konstantin Sergeyev, had been coaching her very carefully for her first performance as Giselle in Leningrad – a major step forward in her career. However after the defection of Nureyev in Paris, the Kirov, on its way to London, needed another star, and so British audiences were the first to see Makarova as Giselle. The result was a triumph: with her long legs and arms, she achieved superb romanticism and individuality, pouring hundreds of nuances into her interpretation.

In 1970, she too defected, seeking (like Nureyev) wider chances of development. Since then, she has had a freelance career, guesting in many countries. For some years, she was a star of American Ballet Theatre, taking leading roles, and developing artistically as she tackled such challenging roles as Caroline in *Jardin aux lilas*. Tudor liked her because she fought back when he needled her, as was his custom. Although he disapproved of her interpretation of some of his

choreography, he said of her, 'We form a mutual admiration society,' and he helped her to stage the fourth act of *La Bayadère* – the Kingdom of the Shades – for American Ballet Theatre.

Her interpretation of Giselle developed in a marvellous way after that evening in 1961. She dropped a number of the musical nuances in which she was coached by Sergeyev, but continued to develop dramatic aspects of the role. Indeed, she kept changing her interpretation of Giselle, just as she continued to change her interpretation of Odette–Odile in *Swan Lake*. Her development of the latter is of special interest. At first, she made a rather simple contrast between the two roles, but after watching a film comparing Ulanova and Plisetskaya as Odette, she was inspired to develop Odette and Odile in a more complex way, stressing the links between the two.

She showed a delightful flair as an actress when she interpreted the leading role of the Russian ballerina in the musical *On Your Toes*, in New York and London. She was very much more than just a presenter when she took part in the excellent BBC series *Ballerina* (1987). She played an important role in shaping the programmes, and her comments showed a warm appreciation of the talents of other ballerinas.

When the Kirov appeared in London in 1988, Makarova made a last-minute appearance in one of their 'divertissements' programmes. This highly emotional occasion was televized live by BBC TV. In 1989 Makarova was invited to perform with the Kirov again, this time in the Soviet Union – she danced two *pas de deux* from Cranko's *Onegin*. Russian audiences were wildly appreciative.

Mikhail Baryshnikov

In many ways, Mikhail Baryshnikov's career followed the pattern set by Nureyev and Makarova. Like them, he was trained at the great school in Leningrad; like them, he was accepted within the Kirov Ballet as an artist of supreme quality; like them, he defected when the Kirov was on tour in the West, in order to achieve wider opportunities; and like them, he was soon accepted in the West as a superstar. However, he has shown, more strongly than either Nureyev or Makarova, a tendency to settle down within one company – partly because his small stature limits his choice of partners. Although he has performed widely as a guest artist, he gave his main allegiance to American Ballet Theatre.

He began his training in Riga, the capital of Latvia where he was born in 1948, but at the age of 15, he moved to Leningrad and became a pupil of the great teacher Pushkin. Baryshnikov already showed rare ability to master all aspects of the classical technique, and Pushkin was able to help him to develop his individual gifts to the full, while teaching him stage-craft and helping him to distinguish between technical expertise and dancing as an art.

Baryshnikov considers that his first performance as Albrecht in *Giselle* in 1972 was the most important of all his debuts in the Soviet Union. Although his rare gifts were recognized, he looked extremely young, and did not fit the accepted image of Albrecht as a noble aristocrat. He found the key to success by interpreting Albrecht in a new way: he showed him as a man who loves Giselle right from the start of the ballet – with a love so deep that he fears to jeopardize it by revealing his true identity to Giselle.

His achievement in a wide variety of roles in the repertoire of American Ballet Theatre was so extraordinary that he became a celebrity far outside the ballet world. He looked especially superb dancing with Gelsey Kirkland and Natalia Makarova, for they were well matched to him in height, perfection of line and technical mastery.

When Tudor restaged his Buddhist masterpiece *Shadowplay* for American Ballet Theatre, he gave the central role to Baryshnikov – and helped him to prepare for it by giving him books on Zen Buddhism to read. This role was a great challenge to him, being quite unlike any he had danced before, but he was delighted to tackle it.

The challenge was also great when, in 1976, Twyla Tharp was inspired by his dancing to create the central role for him in *Push Comes to Shove*, a role which not only did not resemble anything he had tackled before, it was unlike anything she had created before. Although her roots were in modern dance, she used his extraordinary command of the classical ballet technique to quite new effect: he was very funny, and quite unpredictable. Indeed, it sometimes looked as if even he did not know how a leap would end when he took off; he took Twyla Tharp's habit of making a dancer change direction off the beat and gave it a marvellous new substance.

Other choreographers also created roles for him – notably Jerome Robbins and Alvin Ailey. Working with Robbins on *Other Dances* (the sequel to *Dances at a Gathering*) was a revelation to him. Even though the ballet is very demanding – it takes the form of a much-extended *pas de deux* – Baryshnikov learned it at great speed, with Robbins demonstrating everything for him. In the 1977 film *The Turning Point*, he played a role that was partly inspired by his own life, and his acting and dancing in it helped to make him even more famous. Herbert Ross and Nora Kaye intended the leading female role in this film for Gelsey Kirkland – together Baryshnikov and Kirkland were likely to do wonders. Unfortunately, she developed anorexia nervosa, and the film suffered without her in the leading role.

Notwithstanding his honoured position in American Ballet Theatre, he left the company in 1978 to join the New York City Ballet to work with Balanchine. It was only the invitation from Lucia Chase to take over as director that brought him back to American Ballet Theatre in 1980.

Eva Evdokimova

Of all the superstars of the second half of the 20th century, Eva Evdokimova is the most cosmopolitan. Her father is Bulgarian, her mother American, and she was born, in 1948, in Switzerland. Her early training was in Munich, and at the age of 10, she began training at the Royal Ballet School in London. She took a crucial step when she left there to train with Maria Fay at her London studio, for Hungarian-born Maria Fay is a great teacher: fully trained in the Russian 'school' as systematized by Agrippina Vaganova, but developing the Russian 'school' in many ways. Evdokimova developed rapidly under Fay's tuition, perfecting her line, gaining strength and developing superb musicality.

The first ballet company she joined (in 1966) was the Royal Danish Ballet, where she continued her training in the Russian 'school' under Vera Volkova, and also mastered the Bournonville 'school'. At this time, the Royal Danish Ballet assigned solo roles only to Danish dancers, and as a consequence, Evdokimova joined the ballet of the Deutsche Oper in West Berlin in 1969. Her talent was so outstanding that, soon after joining the company, she was allowed to dance the very challenging role of Princess Aurora in *The Sleeping Beauty* – showing a touching fragility made possible by her superb technique. A year later, having reached the age of 21, she decided at the last moment to enter the great international ballet competition in Varna, competing with the finest dancers in the world up to the age of 29, coming from the Soviet Union, Cuba, the United States and many other countries. In the event, the international jury, with Galina Ulanova as president, awarded her gold medal – thus establishing Evdokimova as a dancer of the highest quality.

Later the same year, she danced Giselle for the first time, in Berlin. Yvette Chauviré, one of the greatest Giselles of this century, taught and coached her. It became one of Evdokimova's finest roles, with a very personal interpretation which kept changing in subtle ways.

LEFT *Baryshnikov as Basil in a* pas de deux *from the Petipa ballet* Don Quixote.
RIGHT *Eva Evdokimova as Odette in* Swan Lake, *showing magical* dusha *and romanticism. London Festival Ballet, 1978.*

OVERLEAF LEFT *Rudolf Nureyev (title role) and Eva Evdokimova (Nastasia Filipovna) rounding out their roles in* The Idiot, *choreographed by Valeri Panov in 1979 for the Deutsche Oper Ballet, West Berlin.*
OVERLEAF RIGHT *Evdokimova in the title role of Bournonville's* La Sylphide, *as staged by Peter Schaufuss for London Festival Ballet, and in the same form for the Deutsche Oper Ballet, West Berlin.*

In 1971, she was invited back to Copenhagen to dance the title role of *La Sylphide*, for no Danish dancer would achieve such perfection in the romantic (and sometimes amusing) Bournonville choreography. Her performance, as she danced in the standard version of the ballet as presented (with some cuts) by the Royal Danish Ballet, prepared the way for the later triumph in London in 1977 in Peter Schaufuss's enriched version.

She also danced her first Odette–Odile in 1971, in Berlin, and it was soon added to the growing list of her finest roles. She danced it with that mysterious Russian soulfulness known as *dusha* and with a truly Russian breadth of movement and elevation.

In 1973 in Munich, she danced Juliet for the first time, in Cranko's version. However, as she travelled more and more widely, she found it necessary to master five different versions – including Nureyev's, which she danced in London with the virtuoso himself, in a London Festival Ballet season. The effort of will required to remember five different versions of the same role, to the same music, is hard to imagine – and very typical of this artist, who knows so well how to use her keen intelligence, computer-like memory and extraordinary adaptability.

This adaptability was put to a severe test when Alicia Alonso invited her to Cuba to dance the role of Giselle – a precious tribute from one great artist to another, but one that put Evdokimova under great strain, for Alonso's Giselle had dozens of unique features. To make things worse, the complexities of the international ballet festival in Cuba were such that she had only one morning in which to learn the role. By mischance, Jorge Esquivel (Alonso's regular partner at the time) had injured himself, and was not there. In fact, there was no one to rehearse her. A message was sent to Alonso, who came to the studio and calmly and expertly took Evdokimova through the entire role; even Esquivel turned up, and bravely partnered her, though one knee was wrapped in a huge bandage.

Evdokimova reached a turning point in her career in 1979, when she tackled with great success two roles in which she moved out of romanticism into quite different artistic genres. When Valery Panov created his version of the Dostoyevsky novel *The Idiot* in West Berlin, he gave Evdokimova the very strange and disturbing role of the very vulnerable Nastasia Filipovna, who has been deeply hurt, and so has put a shell around herself, becoming a courtesan. She is strongly attracted to Prince Myshkin (the 'idiot') but has become so self-destructive that she rejects him in favour of the evil Ragozhin. Panov's choreography, based on his years in Soviet ballet, did not encompass all these complexities, but it had many spaces between the steps, and Evdokimova filled them in superbly.

Her experience with the title role of Glen Tetley's *Sphinx*, revived by him for the London Festival Ballet, was quite different. Tetley spoke little in rehearsal, but demonstrated clearly, and in this way, Evdokimova mastered his style, with its fusion of modern dance and ballet, and created a mysterious, powerful, menacing and sensual creature who attempts to seduce Oedipus so that she may destroy him. In this role, she expanded her range of movement, and projected Tetley's entirely personal vision of the ancient Greek myth with splendid authority.

In November 1987, there was a gala programme at the Kirov Theatre, celebrating the 50th anniversary of the day Natalia Dudinskaya joined the company. A number of Kirov dancers, her former pupils, took part, but Dudinskaya – who had taught Evdokimova on numerous occasions, and greatly admired her – insisted that she should be invited, even though she was not a member of the company. Evdokimova responded to this invitation by creating something very special for Dudinskaya; she performed (with a Russian partner) all the dancing and mime of the Sylphide in Act II of the Bournonville ballet, ending with the moving death scene – and won an ovation from the audience.

CHAPTER TWENTY-THREE

Vistas of the Future

From time to time, works are produced which include such novel images, produced with the aid of technology, that they open up vistas of the future. Because they are created by highly skilled professionals, and every detail is polished, they belong to a quite different category from the countless works in mixed media which may be described as 'experimental'. The vistas they open up spread out widely, suggesting much further development, and they differ greatly from each other. They have deep roots in what has gone before, but each of them draws sustenance from the past in a highly individual way.

La Joie de Vivre

Both Hector Hoppin and Anthony Gross, who made the drawings for the British animated film *La Joie de Vivre*, showed an extraordinary feeling for dance. The two girls in their film – shown mainly in outline, though there is a light texture in

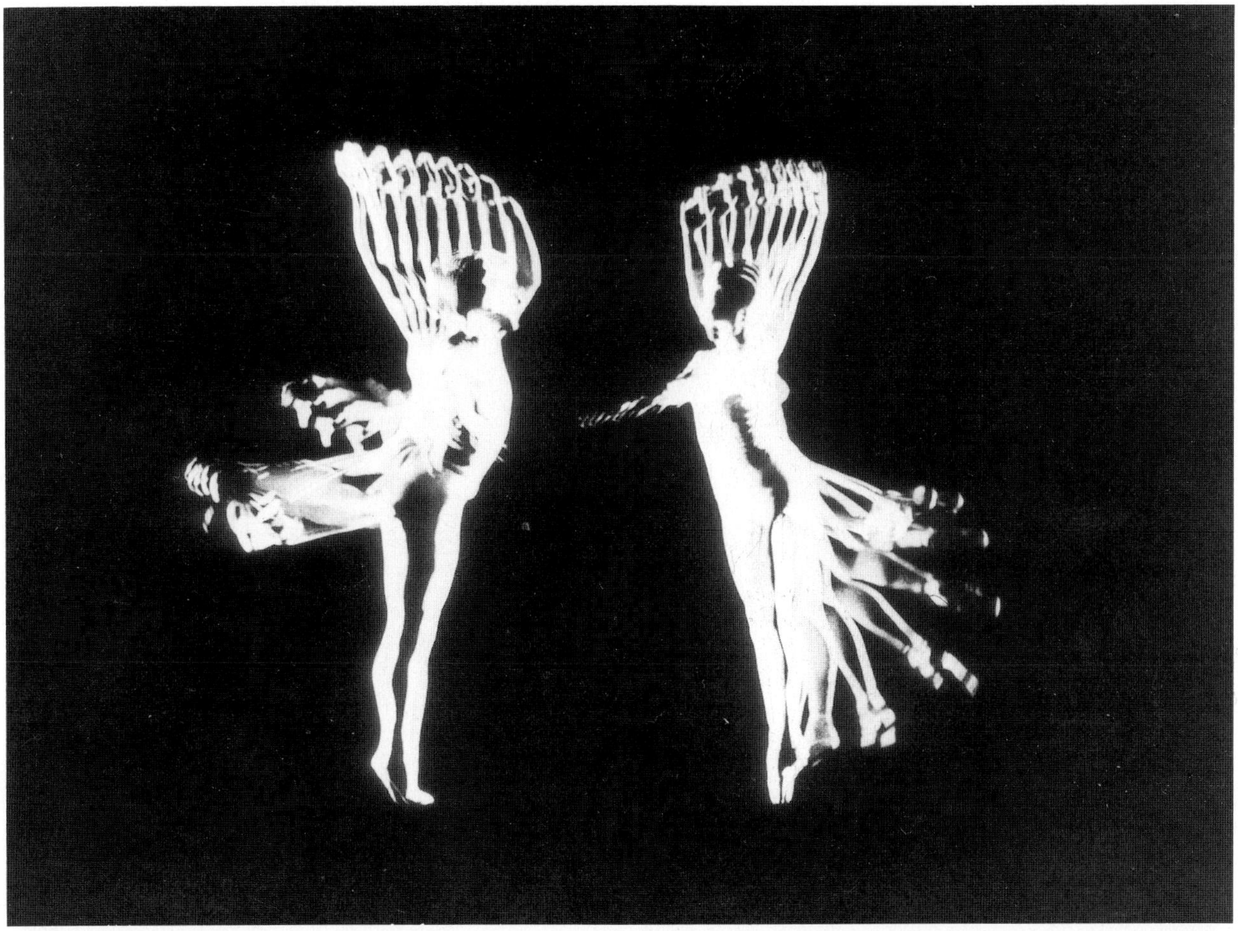

their bodies – move with the grace and lightness of ballerinas, but in a style which is unique: related to human movements, but emphatically different from them. Even their walking movements at the beginning of the film have an amazing freshness and lightness, suggesting the *joie de vivre* of the title, and these qualities become stronger and stronger as they begin to run, leap, dance together and so on. Their skirts, moving in smooth curves allied to those of their bodies, have a life of their own; a somersault, in a smooth slow-motion curve, becomes a dance-image of ravishing beauty. When they dance through the air, in a pond, or on a cable (as tightrope dancers) their movements change in style, while always preserving a delicate exaggeration of the weightlessness which 'live' ballerinas have to work so hard to suggest.

The music, by Tibor Harsanyi, has a delightful transparency, catching exactly the mood of *joie de vivre* intended by the artists. No attempt is made to set the movements exactly to the music – 'mickey-mousing' as it is called by film-makers,

LEFT La Joie de Vivre, *an animated film by Hector Hoppin and Anthony Gross (1934). The girls lean back, holding hands, in a complex leap impossible for live dancers.*

ABOVE Pas de Deux, *a film with choreography by Ludmilla Chiriaeff and images devised by Norman McLaren. The dancers were Margaret Mercier and Vincent Warren from Les Grands Ballets Canadiens. National Film Board of Canada, 1967.*

referring to the precise hitting of the musical beats characteristic of Mickey Mouse films; instead, the two girls float ecstatically above and through the music. This work was created in 1934; and yet it is marvellously contemporary.

Pas de Deux

Norman McLaren, who did so much to develop the art of the animated film while working for the National Film Board of Canada, used 'live' dancers for his film *Pas de Deux*; but he brought all the technical expertise he had acquired over decades of pioneer work in animated films to his treatment of the dancing of the 'live' artists. Ludmilla Chiriaeff, founder-director of Les Grands Ballets Canadiens, provided him with two of her best dancers, Margaret Mercier and Vincent Warren, and choreographed for them a romantic *pas de deux*. McLaren filmed this in slow motion, lighting the dancers from the side, against a black background, so that only the edges of their bodies could be seen. He then proceeded to work for a long time on the 'takes' of the film, so that the

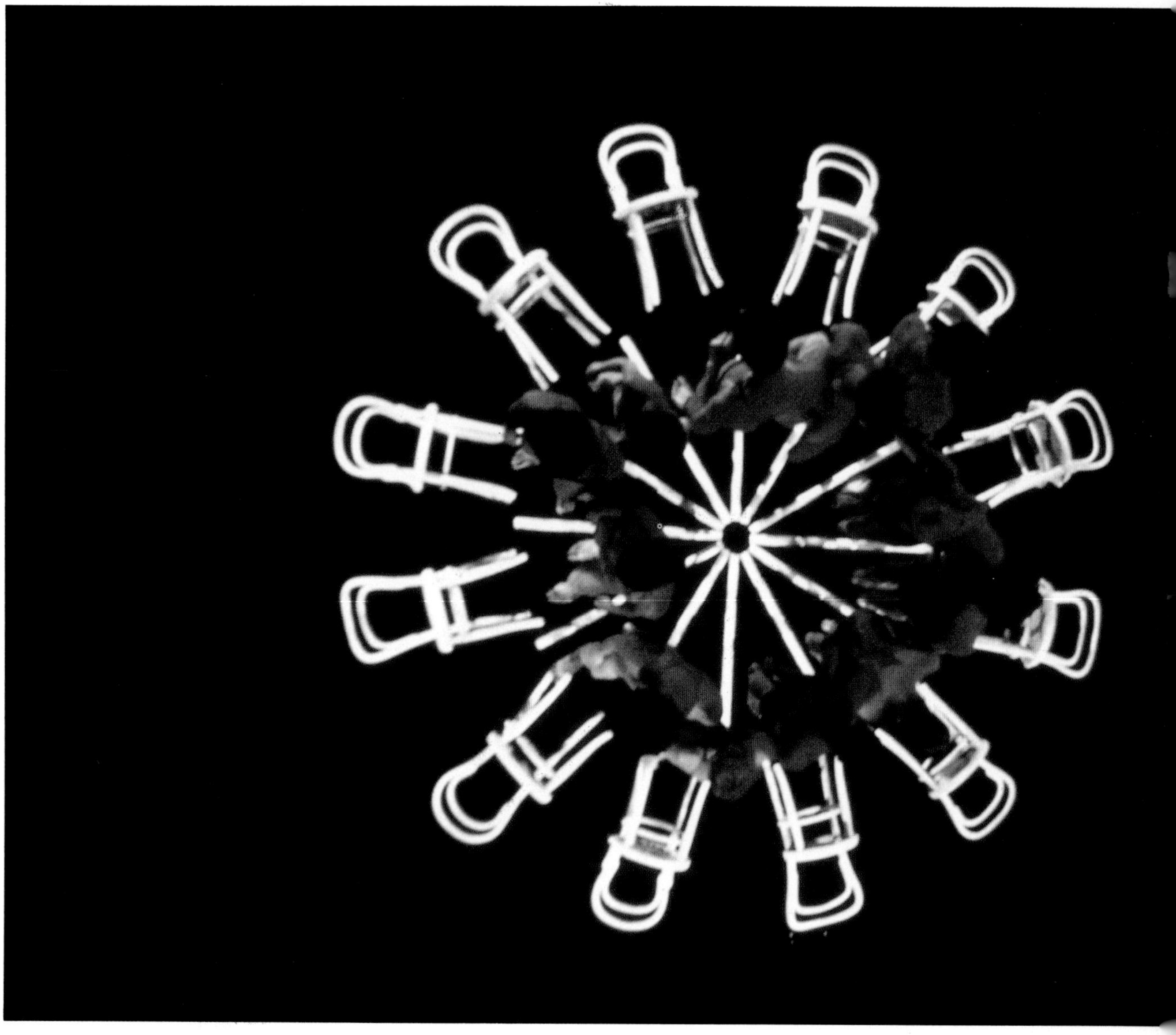

images were utterly transformed, and a mysterious new beauty was born.

The beginning of the film is very simple: the two rim-lit bodies dance slowly and dreamily together. But gradually the images become more and more frieze-like: by repeating certain frames many times, McLaren causes the bodies of the dancers to leave behind a frieze of the outlines of their bodies, stretching out in elegant curves. Using extraordinary imagination and resourcefulness, McLaren keeps bringing in stranger and stranger effects – such as causing a frieze to appear, and making the dancers seem to gather up all the sections of the frieze as they move along it. When the male dancer lifts his partner, the curves overlap in a fascinating way. The musical accompaniment is ideally suited to this slow-motion, very mysterious work: Rumanian folk-music, played slowly on a pan-pipe.

The Relay

When William Fitzwater, a BBC producer/ director, was directing a film about Alwin Nikolais and his work in New York, Nikolais discussed with him his desire to make something *new*, specially for television. Fitzwater liked the idea and the BBC decided to take up Nikolais's suggestion.

The full resources of both film and television were needed, and new electronic equipment had to be constructed for certain effects. Nikolais could not rehearse the choreography for *The Relay* in advance, for he needed to evolve it in full knowledge of the technical facilities which would be in use. In fact, he created it in the long intervals between shots, while the lighting equipment and the camera or cameras were set up in new positions. Following a procedure familiar to him and his dancers, he choreographed with a microphone – telling the dancers exactly what he wanted

LEFT The Relay, *devised and choreographed by Alwin Nikolais for BBC TV. Shot from above, the Nikolais dancers move in a circle in couples, surrounded by overturned chairs (1971).*
ABOVE The Beast, *a television/video piece devised and choreographed by Janet Randell for Lella Productions (1986). Electronically processed, such images suggest the Beast coming up from the sea.*

in each shot; and the dancers responded with characteristic imagination and expertise.

In one particularly imaginative sequence, Nikolais combined film and television techniques in a new way. This is the 'Giacometti scene', in which Nikolais has the dancers stretched out so that they look like figures in sculpture by Giacometti. The film camera was fitted with an anamorphic lens, as used in the CinemaScope process; but Nikolais had it adapted so that it stretched the dancers. Then he went further: he had the film images transformed into video images and further stretched by electronic means.

In another remarkable sequence – 'They came to a city' – Nikolais used two video cameras fitted with zoom lenses, and colour separation overlay (which makes it possible for images from different cameras to be combined in a precise way). The final effect is magical: a group of people walk into a city of towering skyscrapers (actually a model city, filmed by another camera); then the people become larger and larger, while the buildings become smaller, so that the people can look down on them.

There is no overall theme to *The Relay*, but each sequence has its own theme and its own atmosphere, and they combine together with delightful fluidity and surrealist logic.

The Beast

If there is close collaboration between choreographer and director, and the screen images are imaginatively planned, television/video ballets can be just as compelling as the best of stage ballets. They belong to a quite different world from television adaptations of stage ballets; if these are well directed they give pleasure, but inevitably lack the force of imaginative works created from the start for the medium.

Like *The Relay*, *The Beast*, by the English choreographer Janet Randell – transmitted on television and also distributed as a video – was worked out in close collaboration with the director, Hugh David. Unlike Nikolais, Janet Randell used a very strong dramatic theme, a visual projection of a mysterious and frightening passage dealing with the Apocalypse in The Book of Revelation, the last book of the Bible. Drawing on her training in the Lester Horton technique of modern dance at the Alvin Ailey Dance Center in New York, and on her ballet training, Janet Randell uses dancers to create strange and powerful images quite unlike those to be seen in works created for the stage.

The whole screen is suffused with red, and the piece begins with hands and masked faces coming into shot (near the camera) and rapidly retreating. The spoken words from the Bible, accompanying the visual images, describe a beast with seven horns and ten heads: the dancers and the director bring this image to life in a mysterious, semi-abstract way, with moving groups of dancers superimposed on each other, suggesting the heads and horns of the Beast.

In stage works it is hard to combine spoken images and danced images, for the spoken images tend to proceed at a much faster tempo than visual images, and there is less repetition; but television/video techniques make it possible to bring the two types of imagery together, and this is done with admirable control and imagination in *The Beast*.

Vampire–Madonna

The expressionism which flourished in German painting in the early decades of the 20th century was largely inspired by the work of the great pioneer Norwegian painter Edvard Munch, with his deep anxiety and his obsession with women, whom he saw as eternally attractive but also eternally inaccessible and potentially destructive. His paintings include many archetypal images of women; and he also painted many self-portraits showing different aspects of himself as he developed. Munch and his paintings of women and himself therefore provided an ideal theme for a symbolic work, *Vampire–Madonna*, choreographed and danced by the German-born artist, Avis von Herder. In this long solo work, danced in close association with scores of large projections of paintings by Munch, she was able – working in England – to make a new approach to German expressionist modern dance.

Her early training was in classical ballet in Munich; but then she was overwhelmed by the Martha Graham technique, and trained in it, working both in the Martha Graham School in New York and then in Robert Cohan's version of the Graham technique at the London Contemporary Dance School.

In the first half of *Vampire–Madonna* she dances mainly as an adolescent girl, afraid of her first intimations of sexuality and yet dreaming, very tentatively, of coming into sexual contact with a man. Munch has immortalized this figure in his painting of a nude girl, *Puberty*; she also appears as the innocent girl in a white dress in his painting, *Three Stages of Woman*, and Avis von Herder uses a complex montage of projections of Munch's paintings of this archetypal figure. In the second half of the work she symbolizes Munch's erotic ideal: the Madonna-figure, irresistibly seductive and yet also containing some suggestion of menace. A further change of style of dancing and facial expression converts her into the

OPPOSITE Vampire-Madonna, *devised, choreographed and danced by Avis von Herder (1987). Interpreting one of Edvard Munch's obsessions, she dances as a troubled adolescent with a projection of his painting* Puberty.
RIGHT The Ballet Class, *video by teacher/choreographer Maria Fay (at left, demonstrating). At* barre, *in* arabesque penchée, *are Caroline Humpston (left), and Janette Mulligan of London Festival Ballet. Ballet Class Videos, 1986.*

vampire-archetype, erotic yet totally destructive; but there are momentary flashbacks to the innocent girl and the Madonna, maintaining the unity of the work.

Vampire–Madonna shows such profound understanding of Munch and his paintings that Avis von Herder was invited to perform it at the Munch Museum in Oslo and also in a number of Norwegian theatres.

The Ballet Class

For hundreds of years methods of teaching ballet have gradually been perfected by great teachers, so that steps can be performed by dancers with perfect line and rhythm, stamina is developed, and the muscles are gradually warmed up, making it possible for the dancers to tackle more and more difficult steps and *enchaînements*. It is difficult enough to teach dancers, above all in the Russian 'school': this demands profound knowledge of anatomy, psychology and much else. But is it a thousand times more difficult to teach teachers how to use a 'school' to produce fine dancers. A 'school' cannot be encapsulated in a book.

Maria Fay, trained in Budapest in the Russian 'school' (as systematized by Vaganova) by leading Soviet choreographer-teachers, became a star dancer in Hungary, then came to London and established herself as a great teacher, playing a crucial role in the development of such ballerinas as Merle Park, Galina Samsova and Eva Evdokimova. Being also a gifted choreographer – her ballet *Four Romantic Pieces* has become a valuable addition to the repertoire of the Central Ballet of China – she was able to visualize how a 'school' could be passed on in a video, bringing together images and words in a variety of ways, and offering teachers and dancers the chance to study chosen sequences in great detail by using the controls of their video recorders.

Using a group of highly trained dancers – including Janette Mulligan, leading ballerina of the London Festival Ballet – Maria Fay has each exercise of an imaginatively planned class impeccably performed.

Between the exercises she explains their *raison d'être*: what they are intended to achieve, their structure, and their place in the class as a whole. Difficult matters are clarified by close-ups, flashbacks, and so on.

The result is something far more than a video textbook. The exercises, imaginatively composed and beautifully danced, seem like miniature ballets, and Maria Fay speaks and demonstrates with such animation and cogency that she makes the video flow smoothly and sparkle with vitality.

Non-professional lovers of ballet can also enjoy *The Ballet Class*, for it shows in a fascinating way what they do not see on stage – the great underwater mass of the balletic iceberg.

Glossary

adage, adagio The first part of an extended *pas de deux*, in the conventional style established by Petipa, with the ballerina dancing with (and supported by) her partner. Sometimes the *adage* is preceded by the *entrée*. The term is also used for the slow exercises at the beginning of the centre-work of a class, after the *barre*-work is finished.

Anacreontic A term used of a gentle pastoral ballet inspired by a poem by the ancient Greek poet Anacreon.

arabesque A pose in which the dancer stands on one leg, with the other leg behind the body in a fully stretched position. In an *arabesque penchée*, the torso bends forward and the working leg is raised very high so that the back remains arched.

attitude A pose in which the dancer stands on one leg with the other leg raised with knee bent.

ballabile A suite of dances for a large group.

ballerina A *danseuse* who takes leading roles. The term does not appear in the personnel list of British companies: there the term 'principal' covers both ballerinas and senior soloists.

ballet d'action The new type of ballet, with strong dramatic action, created by Hilverding, Angiolini, Noverre and others in the 18th century.

ballet master/mistress In previous centuries, this term signified a choreographer/producer/teacher/company director. Nowadays, it refers to the person who takes the company classes and/or the rehearsals.

balletomane A person who is obsessed with ballet and/or ballet dancers.

Ballettabend In German-speaking countries, where ballets are performed in repertory with operas and sometimes also with plays, a performance confined to ballet is described as a *Ballettabend* ('evening of ballet').

ballonné A step in which the dancer springs up and opens one leg to the front, side or behind, then pulls it back.

ballotté A bouncing step in which the dancer springs up and throws one foot forward, then throws the other foot to the back in a complementary pattern.

barre-work The first part of a class in which the dancers use a bar for help in balancing.

beaten steps Jumping steps in which the lower parts of the legs are beaten together, or past each other. Also known as *batterie*.

block The stiffened front part of a *pointe* shoe.

choreographer The person who composes the choreography. This term and its equivalent in other languages has replaced the older term 'ballet master', but not in Russian.

choreography The movement-text of a ballet or a dance.

choreology The aesthetic and scientific study of human movement through notation. Notators trained at the Benesh Institute of Choreology are commonly known as choreologists.

classic This term is commonly used as a noun to describe a famous ballet created before the beginning of this century. Masterpieces by 20th-century choreographers may be described as 'modern classics'. In the United States, the adjective 'classic' is often used as a synonym for 'classical'.

classical This term is properly used of the ballet technique, perfected by great teachers over the centuries, and of a noble type of dancing and dancers. It is also commonly used to describe all old ballets, but this usage is misleading, since the surviving old ballets are almost all romantic; such ballets could well be described as 'classical-romantic'.

coda The final sections of an extended *pas de deux*, with the two dancers coming together again for a brilliant finale.

contemporary dance A term often used in recent years as a replacement for 'modern dance'. It has been adopted by those teaching the Graham technique, or a technique derived from hers. Both 'modern dance' and 'contemporary dance' are used as technical terms.

contraction An essential part of the Graham technique: one part of the body is contracted, usually suddenly.

corps de ballet Dancers in a company who perform in groups.

coupé A step in which there is a change of weight from one foot to the other. One foot 'cuts' the other and takes its place. A *coupé-jeté* is a leaping step from one foot to the other, following a *coupé*. In *coupé-jeté en tournant*, the step is combined with a turn, and there is a high leap.

dance-image A sequence of movements which together form a memorable passage of choreography, and which choreographers use for expressive purposes.

danseur A male dancer.

danseur noble A male dancer who excels in the noble, classical styles.

danseuse A female dancer.

demi-caractère Used of dancing which employs the classical technique, but which tends to stress comedy and real-life situations, rather than nobility. Also used of adaptations of national folk dances, employing the classical ballet technique.

divertissement A dance not closely associated with the action of a ballet. It relaxes tension for a time, thus paving the way for a further development of the action. There may also be a long suite of *divertissements* intended to entertain (i.e. 'divert' the audience).

duende The dark, mysterious quality projected – when in form – by flamenco dancers and *cante jondo* singers.

dusha A Russian word which can be translated as 'soul', 'feeling', or 'heart'. It is used of the mysterious poetry strongly projected by great dancers trained in the Russian school. It also carries the suggestion of flow.

elevation Height in a leap. To be distinguished from *ballon* – the illusion created by a dancer that he or she is floating through the air, unaffected by gravity.

enchaînement A sequence of steps.

entrée Entrance of ballerina and partner in an extended *pas de deux*.

étoile At the Paris Opéra, where dancers are strictly classified in a long series of ranks, dancers of the top rank are known as *étoiles* (stars).

expressionism An artistic style which, in Germany, is distinguished by an attempt at violent expression by means of exaggeration and distortion. Often there is an element of hysteria or madness, and there is often an evocation of death. Outside Germany, these qualities tend to be less pronounced, and evocations of death are more rare.

fouetté A term used of any step that is 'whipped'. The famous '32 *fouettés*' refer to a series of turns on the spot, with the raised leg doing the whipping.

Intendant The director of an opera house in a German-speaking country. He is in charge of both the opera and the ballet companies. In English-speaking countries, the equivalent term is 'director', 'general director' or 'director-general'.

jeté A jump from one foot to the other.

libretto The story of a ballet.

maître de ballet *See* ballet master.

manège A sequence of steps performed around the stage.

mark In rehearsal, or in class, it is common for the choreographer, producer or coach to ask the dancers to mark the steps, i.e. perform them in a sketchy fashion, in order to save energy.

modern dance New styles of dancing, based on new techniques, which developed in the 20th century as an alternative to ballet and the ballet technique.

pas de deux, pas de trois, pas de quatre, etc. Dances for two, three, four, etc. dancers. In a Petipa ballet, the extended *pas de deux* takes the form of *entrée*, *adage*, man's variation, ballerina's variation, *coda*.

plié A bending of the knee or knees.

pirouette A complete turn, or series of turns, with the body balanced on one toe.

point, pointe The stretched foot. With a full *pointe* the *danseuse* rests on the tip of a blocked shoe. Other positions are the half-*pointe*, and the three-quarter *pointe*, referring to different degrees of stretching, while the body is resting on the toe.

pointe work Dancing on the *pointe*.

release An important part of the Graham technique: one part of the body returns to normal after a contraction.

régisseur Producer.

romantic, romanticism Ballets which reflect the writing style prevalent in the early 19th century, which stressed the supernatural and the exotic. Ballets that are sentimental and emotional are sometimes called 'romantic'.

school A style and technique of dancing, usually perfected by generations of great teachers working in one country. The most famous schools are the old French, the Bournonville (a variant of the old French school), the Italian (with the Cecchetti Method as one branch of it) and the Russian.

staccato Used of movements that are detached from each other.

step A short sequence of movements making up a clearly defined whole – the equivalent of a word in a sentence.

superimposition In television and video, the blending of images from two or more cameras.

storyboard Sketches used by film and television directors to plan what is shown in each shot.

Tour en l'air A turn in the air.

travesti A *danseuse* performing as a man, in a male costume, is described as dancing *en travesti.*

variation A solo dance.

vision mixer The person who controls the succession of images from one camera to another, in television.

Choreographers and a Selection of their Works

Ailey, Alvin
Revelations
Akesson, Birgit
Eye: Sleep in Dream; *Minor Seconds, Major Sevenths*
Alonso, Alberto
Carmen; O-Ye-Ye-O
Alonso, Alicia
Gran Pas de Quatre (reconstruction of Perrot ballet)
Angiolini, Gasparo
Don Juan; *Orfeo ed Euridice* (dance-scenes in opera); *Semiramide*
Ashton, Sir Frederick
Façade; *Les Rendezvous*; *Les Patineurs*; *Symphonic Variations*; *La Fille mal gardée*; *A Month in the Country*
Balanchine, George
Apollo; *The Prodigal Son*; *Serenade*; *Theme and Variations*; *Bourrée fantasque*; *Agon*
Barr, Margaret
The Three Sisters
Béjart, Maurice
The Rite of Spring; *Boléro*; *Romeo and Juliet*; *Bakhti*; *Nijinsky, Clown of God*; *Songs of a Wayfarer*; *The Kabuki, 47 Samurai*; *Seven Greek Dances*
Börlin, Jean
L'Homme et son désir; *La Création du monde*; *Skating Rink*
Bournonville, August
La Sylphide (Sylfiden); *Conservatoire*; *Napoli*; *Kermesse in Bruges*; *A Folk Tale*
Bruce, Christopher
Ghost Dances; *The World Again*
Caciuleanu, Gigi
Equinoxe; *Quarto*; *News*; *Pomodoro Kosmos*
Carter, Jack
Witch Boy
Chase, Alison (with Moses Pendleton)
Shizen
Chiriaeff, Ludmilla
Pas de Deux (film/animation ballet)
Chladek, Rosalia

Symphonie Wien (film ballet)
Coralli, Jean
Giselle (first version, excluding dances and mime of Giselle and Albrecht)
Cranko, John
Pineapple Poll; *Romeo and Juliet*; *Jeu de Cartes*; *Onegin*; *Taming of the Shrew*
Cullberg, Birgit
Miss Julie
Cunningham, Merce
Variations V; *Suite by Chance*
Dai Ai-Lian
The Flying Apsaras
Dauberval, Jean
La Fille mal gardée
De Mille, Agnes
Rodeo
Didelot, Charles-Louis
Flore et Zéphire; *Raoul de Créquis*; *The Prisoner of the Caucasus*
Dolin, Anton
Le Pas de Quatre (reconstruction of Perrot ballet)
Dynalix, Paulette
Two Coppélias
Fay, Maria
Four Romantic Pieces
Flindt, Flemming
The Lesson
Fokine, Mikhail
Le Cygne (The Dying Swan); *Chopiniana (Les Sylphides)*; *Le Pavillon d'Armide*; *Polovstian Dances from Prince Igor*; *Le Carnaval*; *Schéhérazade*; *Cléopâtre*; *The Firebird*; *Le Spectre de la rose*; *Petrushka*
Galeotti, Vincenzo
The Caprices of Cupid and the Ballet Master
Graham, Martha
Lamentation; *Primitive Mysteries*; *El Penitente*; *Frontier*; *Appalachian Spring*; *Night Journey*; *Diversion of Angels*; *Letter to the World*; *Seraphic Dialogue*; *Acrobats of God*
Grigorovich, Yuri
Spartacus
Gross, Anthony
Joie de Vivre (with Hector Hoppin)
Helpmann, Robert
Hamlet
Herder, Avis von
Vampire-Madonna
Herrara, Gustavo
Electra Garrigó
Hilverding, Franz
Pygmalion; *Le Turc généreux*
Holder, Geoffrey
Dougla
Hoppin, Hector
Joie de Vivre (with Anthony Gross)
Horton, Lester
Salome; *The Rite of Spring*; *Conquest*
Humphrey, Doris
Air on a G String; *The Shakers*
Ivanov, Lev
Coppélia; *Polovstian Dances from Prince Igor*; *The Nutcracker*; *Swan Lake (Acts II and IV)*
Jobe, Tom
Liquid Assets; *Run Like Thunder*; *Rite Electrik*
Joffrey, Robert
Astarte
Jooss, Kurt
Petrushka; *The Prodigal Son*; *Pulcinella, The Green Table*; *Big City*
Kai Tai Chan
The Shrew
Kylián Jiří
Symphony in D; *Forgotten Land*; *Sinfonietta*; *Overgrown Path*; *Svadebka*; *Stamping Ground*; *L'Enfant et les sortilèges*
Lander, Harald
Etudes
Lavrovsky, Leonid
Romeo and Juliet
Lester, Keith
Le Pas de Quatre (reconstruction of Perrot ballet)
Limón, José
The Moor's Pavane
Lopukhov, Fyodor
Tanzsymphonia
MacMillan, Kenneth
The Invitation; *Romeo and Juliet*; *Manon*; *Mayerling*
Massine, Leonide
The Three-Cornered Hat; *Pulcinella*; *The Rite of Spring*; *Le Beau Danube*; *Choreartium*; *La Symphonie fantastique*; *Petrushka*
Mendez, Alberto
Tarde en la siesta; *La Diva*
Mitchell, Arthur
Giselle
Nijinska, Bronislava
Les Noces; *Les Biches*
Nijinsky, Vaslav
L'Après-Midi d'un Faune; *Le Sacre du Printemps (The Rite of Spring)*; *Tyl Eulenspiegel*
Nikolais, Alwin
Tent; *The Relay* (television ballet)
Noverre, Jean-George
Jason et Medée; *Les Amours de Henri IV, Antoine et Cléopâtre*
Panov, Valeri
The Idiot
Pavlova, Anna
Autumn Leaves
Pendleton, Moses (with Alison Chase)
Shizen

Perrot, Jules
Giselle; *Le Pas de Quatre*
Petipa, Marius
La Bayadère; *The Sleeping Beauty*; *Swan Lake* (Acts I and III); *Raymonda*
Petit, Roland
Les Demoiselles de la nuit; *Carmen*; *Le Loup*
Plisetskaya, Maya
Anna Karenina
Quirey, Belinda
Orphée et Euridice (dances in the opera)
Randell, Janet
The Beast (television/video ballet)
Robbins, Jerome
Fancy Free; *Afternoon of a Faun*; *The Concert*; *Moves*; *West Side Story* (dances in the musical); *Dances at a Gathering*; *Other Dances*
Saint-Léon, Arthur
Coppélia
Sallé, Marie
Pygmalion; *Bacchus et Ariane*; *Terpsicore*
Schilling, Tom
Elective Affinities
Schlemmer, Oskar
Triadic Ballet
Shankar, Uday
Krishna and Radha
Skeaping, Mary
Flore et Zéphyr (reconstruction of Didelot ballet)
Sokolov, Anna
Rooms; *Deserts*
Staff, Frank
Czernyana; *Peter and the Wolf*; *Transfigured Night*; *Romeo and Juliet*
Taglioni, Filippo
La Sylphide
Taylor, Paul
Three Epitaphs; *Aureole*; *Party Mix*; *Orbs*, *Private Domain*
Tenorio, Iván
Hamlet
Tetley, Glen
Pierrot Lunaire; *Mythical Hunters*; *Embrace Tiger and Return to Mountain*; *Sphinx*
Tharp, Twyla
Push Comes to Shove
Tudor, Antony
Jardin aux lilas; *Dark Elegies*; *Gala Performance*; *Judgement of Paris*; *Pillar of Fire*; *Romeo and Juliet*; *Undertow*; *Shadow of the Wind*; *Echoing of Trumpets*; *The Divine Horsemen*; *Shadowplay*; *Knight Errant*; *The Leaves Are Fading*
Valois, Dame Ninette de
The Rake's Progress; *Checkmate*
Vasiliev, Vladimir
Anyuta
Viganò, Salvatore
The Creatures of Prometheus; *Gli Strelizzi*; *I Titani*; *Dedalo e Icare*; *Otello*; *Giovanna d'Arco*
Weaver, John
The Loves of Mars and Venus; *Orpheus and Eurydice*
Weidman, Charles
Lynch Town; *The Unicorn in the Garden*
Wigman, Mary
The Dance of Death; *Hexentanz* (Witch Dance)
Zakharov, Rotislav
The Fountain of Bakhchisarai

Index

Figures in italics refer to captions